Over The Hill
At 40
And Other
Outrageous
Lies

by

Florence and Al Tauber

THIRD AGE PRESS
1075 S.W. Murray Road, Suite 277
Portland, OR 97229-9906

Dedication

To Florence and the image ♡♡ that started it all.

We linked our hearts together and entered into the adventure of life. By being real, and exposing your innermost feelings, you helped me understand the true nature of human nature.

✳ ✳ ✳

To Al who gave me my childhood and created the climate for me to grow in. Whose expectations of me exceeded my own and who was always, always there applauding.

✳ ✳ ✳

For Andy, Denise and Kellie Elizabeth who add so much to our lives. And for Alan, our grandson, for whom we strive to do our part in helping to create a culture in which the world is a place of love, beauty and growth.

Acknowledgments

To the following authors, researchers, publications, and organizations whose groundbreaking works created the soil and climate in which this book was sown and grew.

James L. Adams, American Association of Retired Persons, American Psychological Association, Jefferey Blumberg, Walter M. Bortz II, M.D., George Burns, Robert N. Butler, M.D., Mary Baird Carlsen, Rebecca Chalker, Walter J. Cheney, Colonial Penn Insurance Group, Alex Comfort, The Commonwealth Fund, Dr. Kenneth Cooper, Malcolm Cowley, Lawrence M. Crapo, William J. Diehm, Paula Brown Doress, Ken Dychtwald, Ph.D., William Evans, Ph. D., James F. Fries, David Hackett Fisher, Joe Flower, Peter Gorner, Thomas Hager, Marvin Harris, Martha Holstein, Paul Homer, Frederic M. Hudson, Pricilla W. Johnson, Journal of the American Society on Aging, Laureen Kessler, Ronald Kotulak, Lears, Caroline Bird Little, Elissa Halamed, Ph.D., Rochelle Myers, Muriel Oberleder, Ph.D., Dr. Dean Ornish, Pat O'Shea, Michael Ray, Irwin H. Rosenberg, Elyse Salend, Frank E. Seeley, SeniorNet, Diana Laskin Siegel, Carole Sinclair, B.F. Skinner, U.S. Administration on Aging. U.S. Department of Labor, M.E. Vaughan, Kristene E. Whitmore, Marlene Wilson, Melanie Astaire Witt.

Warning—Disclaimer

This book is designed to provide information in regard to the subject matter covered. It is sold with the understanding that the publisher and authors are not engaged in rendering legal, accounting or other professional services. If legal or other expert assistance is required, the services of a competent professional should be sought.

It is not the purpose of this work to reprint all the information that is otherwise available to the author and/or publisher, but to complement, amplify and supplement other texts. You are urged to read all the available material, learn as much as possible about ideas in aging and to tailor the information to your individual needs.

Every effort has been made to make this book as complete and as accurate as possible. However, there may be mistakes both typographical and in content. Therefore, this text should be used only as a general guide to aging information.

The purpose of this book is to educate and entertain. The authors and Third Age Publishing shall have neither liability nor responsibility to any person or entity with respect to any loss or damage caused, or alleged to be caused, directly or indirectly by the information contained in this book.

Table Of Contents

Imagine

I magine a society in which 80 out of 100 of its members live to an average age of 85 (see Figures 1 and 2), vigorous and vital, and die a natural death. A visionary dream, impractical, unrealistic? Not at all, with the advances in health care, nutrition and age retardation, a longer life is not only possible, but inevitable.

So, imagine a world in which:

Life has not only been prolonged for the average person, but for every one in 10,000 the span of years is extended to 110.

There is a positive view of aging and those

in their mature years are valued for their wisdom, creativity, and contributions.

"Third Age" people are respected members of the community and active participants in business, industry, government and volunteer organizations.

Men live almost as long as women and both live well.

Financially sound, mature women are sought after for their vibrancy, health, wisdom, and sexuality.

It is recognized that functional age has nothing to do with chronological age.

Technology and assistive devices are used by everyone to increase, maintain or improve functional capabilities that decline with age, such as vision and hearing.

Work, either paid or volunteered, is respected for its contribution to longevity and vitality.

The Third Age is focused on creative endeavors which encourage late bloomers to live to the maximum of their outer limits.

The disabled are full participants in society with their independence, control, contributions, and dignity fully respected.

The authors of this book are presenting the immediate future to readers who wish to have more control over their mature years and need reliable information to do so. There are a lot of myths about aging in our society. In a straightforward manner this book dispels most of them.

It is a book of anecdotes, facts, inspiration

and suggestions about the challenges of becoming older. In addition, the book contains a convenient catalog of works available to the reader who wants to know more about a particular subject on aging. Sex beyond sixty, strength training for the mature, hormones to retard the aging process, social security limitations in the present system, control of incontinence—these are just a few of the topics you can read about in *Over The Hill At 40 and Other Outrageous Lies.*

The central message in this book is that aging does not have to mean decrepitude. Those who wish to stay vital can do so much longer than they dreamed if they follow the few suggestions we've made here. The largest part of staying healthy and vigorous is your state of mind. You have to agree to adopt a new way of thinking about age and forego destructive behavior which is not only permitted but encouraged in our present society. You can help change that and live longer in better health if you choose to do so.

Good luck.

Figure 1: James F. Fries and Lawrence M. Crapo, in their book Vitality and Aging (Catalog) demonstrated that the health span could be extended and the decline of vitality slowed. Figure 1 demonstrates that by following some simple rules most people could extend their vital years to an average of 85, and one in 10,000 could live to 110 years. It shows what would happen if contagious diseases are eliminated and chronic diseases are either eliminated or postponed.

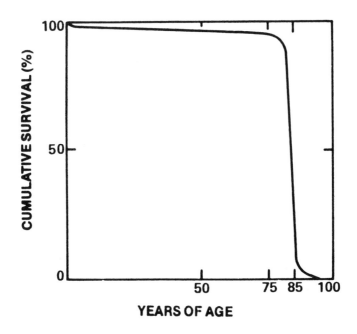

THE RECTANGULAR SURVIVAL CURVE

Figure 1
The initial dip following birth represents infant mortality. The slow decline from age one to about age 70 demonstrates the small percentage of deaths occurring during those years. After age 75, the curve makes a sharp downward turn, and after only a few more years nearly all the members of the population have died. Finally, the curve slackens to represent those few individuals surviving to very old ages.

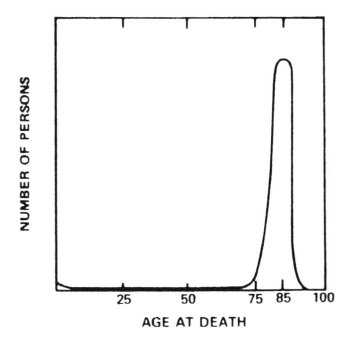

Figure 2

Ideal mortality curve in the absence of premature death. The average death occurs at age 85, with a standard deviation of about four years. Ninety-five percent of all deaths occur between the ages of 77 and 93. (U. S. Bureau of Health Statistics).

Printed with permission from *Vitality And Aging,* Copyright 1981 W.H. Freeman.

Introduction

The ideas upon which this book is based are very simple:

1. We are programmed just like computers by our youth oriented culture into an aging myth.

2. We buy the myth and behave in accordance with its dictates.

3. Most studies of aging survey populations that have bought into the myth and, as a result find evidence to support it.

4. The myth is a lie.

5. At any age there are a great number of things you can do to improve your health span,

vitality, and longevity.

6. There is an overwhelming body of scientific evidence that demonstrates that you can function, mentally and physically, 20-30 years younger than you are.

7. The impact of the myth (ageism) is much, much harder on women than on men.

8. As the civil rights and feminist movements have demonstrated it is possible to modify our society and reduce the impact of any ism.

9. To modify our society's attitudes on ageism four things have to take place:

A. The existence of the ageism has to be verbalized and exposed.

B. Organizations have to come into being dedicated to elimination of ageism.

C. Laws have to be passed setting up legal sanctions against ageism.

D. The population affected must become actively involved in demanding their rights. We all have to dedicate ourselves to eliminating ageism.

10. With ageism the first three have taken place. Now it's up to you to aggressively exercise the various powers you have to bring an end to ageism.

11. Your powers are:

A. Personal Power—The power to modify your own behavior, reject the myth and behave to maximize your life expectancy and vitality.

B. Purchasing Power—The power to boycott advertisers and retailers that perpetuate the myth.

C. Political Power—The power to elect representatives who will continue to pass legislation favorable to the Third Age.

D. Financial Power—Which we all must achieve to protect ourselves from the inevitable erosion of promised social security and retirement benefits because of the sheer numbers in the Third Age population.

We have an opportunity to both change ourselves and change society. It does take commitment and discipline to reap the harvest of continuing vitality, a long healthy span, and a short disability period leading to death. We have assembled the proof statements behind these bold assertions. Because women and men age and feel differently this book had to be written by a woman and a man so that both viewpoints could be expressed.

Myths

C ultural anthropology teaches us that we are
born as blank slates. The accident of birth
puts us into a particular culture that
programs us into its belief systems, values and
isms. While anthropologists try not to make value
judgements on cultures they agree that those which
bring less stress on their members are preferred. In
"Perspectives on Aging: Exploding the Myth," a
lecture series funded by the Colonial Penn
Insurance Group these issues were explored at
Duke University and the Universities of Southern
California, Michigan, and Washington.

Each University has a highly respected gerontological center which has contributed significantly to current knowledge of the aging process. Researchers have agreed that the definition of who is considered "elderly" is determined by the culture, which varies from society to society. In some societies the elderly are not defined by chronological age, but by some achieved status such as becoming a grandparent, or becoming head of a clan, or being appointed to a council of elders. Other societies define the elderly as those who are no longer physically or mentally competent to carry out normal activities.

It's the Western societies, in contrast, that define the elderly as those over age 65, regardless of achieved status or competence. We often forget that in other cultures the aged are the most powerful, the most engaged, and the most respected members of the society.

As an example, Frenchmen appreciate older women. They value them for their vibrancy, health, wisdom, and sexuality.

We have little reason to believe in the mores of the American society which have so often been proven wrong, such as smoking, not exercising, alcohol abuse, improper dietary practices, stress and the long list of isms.

What is Normal? We tend to define normal by what is popular rather than what could be. If a culture's lifestyle is in error, as ours has been in terms of aging, diet, and exercise, all our measurements and published data about the organism are suspect. What would the data be if it were based on a population that lived on its physical, emotional intellectual and creative outer limits? Much different! Just as racial groups suffer from racism and women suffer from sexism, the aged in our society suffer from ageism, prejudice and discrimination against the aged.

Slang epithets for older persons are widely used: dirty old man, old geezer, old codger, old maid, old biddy, old hag, senile, and decrepit.

Health care workers in general have negative attitudes towards the elderly. That is because their focus is on curing rather than on long term treatment.. Their attitudes tend to focus on perceived deterioration.

Only one in 50 persons single out the later years as the best time of a person's life.

Discrimination against the older person is dependent on the fact that the undesirable trait, his or her old age, can be easily observed. As a result of these prejudices and discriminations, most older persons tend to deny their age, and try to camouflage it, and suffer from lowered self-esteem when they have to admit their age.

Greeting card counters are filled with birthday cards that joke about adding another year, and often about physical and sexual decline.

Ageism harms the young as well as the old. When young people develop a negative view of aging and of older persons, they may lower their goals for achievement in later life.

We know there are few, if any, inevitable declines in physical and mental functioning as we grow older. The Third Age population can operate at the same level with which it has functioned in younger years and in some cases, better.

In order to conserve the value of older individuals, we have to replace the ageism myth with a new belief system. We have to reprogram ourselves to focus on functional age rather than chronological age. We must all fight the myth recognizing that our sheer numbers and the exercise of our purchasing power and political power can change the world as it now is to a welcoming and respectful place.

The term Ageism was developed by Robert N. Butler, M.C., the first Director of the National Institute of Aging in 1968. In his book *Why Survive* which received a Pulitzer Prize he described ageism as:

"Ageism can be seen as a process of systematic stereotyping of and discrimination against people because they are old, just as racism and sexism accomplish this with skin color and gender. Old people are categorized as senile, rigid in thought and manner, old-fashioned in morality and skills. Ageism allows the younger generation to see older people as different from themselves; thus they subtly cease to identify with their elders as human beings."

Television

A recent 195-page report is the result of five years of research by the American Psychological Association's Task Force on Television and Society. It reported that:

The elderly watch television more than any other age group. For some isolated older Americans viewing becomes a "parasocial activity" that helps maintain "the illusion of living in a populated world." Television often fills gaps left by the death of a spouse or the distancing of a grown family.

Elderly viewers watch news, documentaries and public-affairs programs.

The task force found that television portrayals have often reinforced negative stereotypes of racial and ethnic minorities and of women. The model female character on television is still a beautiful young adult, valued more for her appearance than her capabilities and competence. Watching television can lead to anti-social behavior, obesity, gender and racial stereotyping, and lack of self esteem.

The report recommends that the federal government develop a national "television policy" to promote "quality" and diverse programming and to "protect citizens and society from harmful effects."

Elyse Salend, director of a television-industry survey by the University of California, Los Angeles, (UCLA) reported that the TV industry is shortchanging older viewers in terms of the number and quality of programs geared toward a mature audience. More than 1500 members (24%) of the Academy of Television Arts and Sciences told researchers of industry wide ageism in programming and employment. Here are some of the survey's key findings:

Half believe that older adults are portrayed unrealistically, and 65 percent think their industry characterizes the concerns of older persons poorly.

Eighty-five percent agreed there would be more elders on screen if advertisers directed more products to the over-50 market.

Even though three in four persons in the survey said they plan to work past age 65 and agreed that their lives have improved with added years, an overwhelming 87 percent asserted that their industry considers persons 65 and older "over the hill." Further, 47 percent reported becoming more anxious about the future with increased age. Almost half of the respondents had experienced age discrimination in the television industry, with 59 percent of these persons saying they had been considered too old.

Survey participants indicated that professional groups most likely to experience job discrimination because of advanced years were performers, writers, and directors. Salend's conclusion was that the television industry is out of step with our maturing society. She reported that by 2030, one third of the U.S. population will be age 55 or older, up from the current 20 percent. The study was funded by the U.S. Administration on Aging. For information contact Elyse Salend at (310)206-5223.

Another survey of 6,000 women with an average age of 59 and a range of 56 to 70 revealed that 89 percent of the respondents felt advertising and promotional messages cater to younger working women and mothers. About 96 percent of the older women feel the fashion industry ignores their changing needs.

Older women are defecting from television network daytime serials with 79 percent reporting the story lines completely ignore subjects that interest them. More than 85 percent have shifted their prime-time viewing from networks to three preferred alternatives: CNN, PBS and the Discovery Channel.

Alex Comfort says in *A Good Age* "One national show which represents older Americans keeping their end up and fighting put-downs, and one national magazine with programs by and for seniors, could achieve more in less time than a constitutional amendment asserting the right to be decently treated as you get older. You could start pressing for them now."

Retiring

R etiring is probably the greatest myth that has been perpetuated on the American public and probably does the most harm. One has to recognize that retirement is a political device imposed by one group on another for the purposes of control.

Retiring was invented by Prince Otto von Bismark in 1883, when he established the world's first state system of social security in order to weaken the appeal of socialism. He set retirement age at 70 and did not expect that the average worker would ever receive a pension, since life expectancy in Germany at that time was about 45. German officials later reduced the retirement age to 65.

The selection of age 65 for use as a demarcation between middle and old age was an arbitrary one. It had nothing to do with a person's ability to work. This numerical definition of old age has been adhered to for social purposes and as a means for determining the point of eligibility for various services for older people. Employment should be a matter of choice after 65.

One third of retirees reenter the job market within two years of retirement. Blue collar workers go back most likely for financial reasons, while white collar employees are more likely to reenter because they enjoy their work.

The ability to work is hampered by the earnings limits for recipients of social security. The earnings limit was established, as a matter of public policy to drive older people out of the labor force to make way for younger workers. That need no longer exists and it is detrimental to the person who needs to work to live.

The policy was very effective. In 1948 one half of all American men 65 plus worked, in 1989 only 16 percent.

The Third Age population should aggressively pressure Congress and the President to remove earnings restrictions and recognize the multiple benefits that a Third Age labor force brings to the market place. Among them are contributions to taxes and reduction in health care costs resulting from a more vital older population.

In 1935 when our social security system was established 65-year-olds lived 12.5 years longer. Our politicians made a generous social security offer to workers just like Bismark, predicated on the fact that very few would live to take advantage of it. Now 72-year-olds will live 12.5 years longer. As a result, our government now faces the inability to keep its promises and we can expect only a continual reduction of benefits over time. This is another battle that the Third Age population has to prepare to fight vigorously.

One of the organizations leading that battle is the National Committee to Preserve Social Security and Medicare, 2000 K Street, N.W. Washington D.C. 20006. They need your membership and your dollars. For your money you will receive their regular newspaper, *Saving Social Security* as well as legislative alerts suggesting ways you can actively participate when something vital is about to happen in Congress affecting your Social Security and Medicare benefits.

In addition they have a telephone hotline "Senior Flash" (202)822-9187, that will provide you with weekly updates on what's going on in the House and Senate.

By joining you will be adding your weight to eleven million citizens who have shown their support for the National Committee by writing letters, signing petitions and supporting various campaigns. The committee reports that President Bush's 1992 budget includes a five year $13.8 billion slash in Medicare services.

At this writing, Congress was evaluating

proposals by Senators Domenici, Rudman, Nunn, Robb and President Bush to impose arbitrary spending caps on Medicare and other entitlement programs. This was a major effort on the part of the administration to break its contract with the Third Age population.

Yet science and medicine long has recognized that age has only limited relevance to the general function, health, mental capacity, physical endurance and creativity of people. Throughout life, age is only a convenient and inaccurate indication of a person's physical and mental status.

When our country was an agricultural society few retired. But as we have become more industrialized the idea of rewarding labor with leisure benefits after a fixed employment period became public policy. And it was effective. Look at the figures: In 1900, 70 percent of men over 65 were employed. Sixty years later in 1960 only 35 percent were employed after 65. By 1975 only 22 percent were working and in 1983 only 17 percent.

Indicative of the negative impact of retiring is the high suicide rate for aged men. The figures show that the suicide rate of men 55 to 64 is 22.5 per 100,000 from 65 to 74 - 28.4, from 75 to 84 - 41.4, 85 and over 50.2. A total of 37,000 men over the age 65 killed themselves in the period 1980 to 1986.

Both white and blue collar workers suffer from loss of self-esteem if they don't have a consuming activity to absorb them after retirement. The solution is to retire into work and start another career or volunteer for worthwhile activities.

Alex Comfort, Author of *A Good Age* reports that only two kinds of folk are really happy conventionally retired: Those who were always lazy, and those who have waited a lifetime to devote themselves to a consuming, non-fantasy interest for which they have studied, prepared and planned, lacking only the time to do it the way they wanted.

Beginning in the late 1980s the trend of retiring at 65 reversed. According to records of the U.S. Bureau of Labor Statistics in 1988 among men age 60, 68.8 percent were still in the work force. The next year the percentage had jumped to 70.7 and has stayed there. Profound changes in American society have caused the reversal. Among them is the factor that married couples are putting off starting a family, leaving them with children to raise when they reach early retirement age.

There are other economic forces at work. Generous early retirement incentives, popular in the 1980's as a payroll-cutting device, are reported to be declining. Even more crucial is the fact that employers are shifting more and more of the cost of retiree health insurance to employees, giving middle-aged workers a strong incentive to stay on the job.

The Economics Of Aging

The fact of the matter is that retirement is not a practical goal for the majority of people given the economics of living longer. As you get older you will find your income curving downward if it is not augmented by additional income. Two out of five older persons, some 12 million people, live in poverty or close to its edge. The proportion of retirees receiving private pension income increased to 16.9 percent in 1990. Only a tiny fraction of these pensions are indexed to protect against inflation. These are the persons considered to be retirement winners. The wealthiest 20 percent prospered the most, getting nearly half of all elderly income; the poorest one fifth got less than 4 percent.

Two million women who live alone are below the poverty line. While 3.7 million older persons are officially declared poor, another 8.1 million are considered near poor. Any sudden economic reversal could push them into poverty. Altogether, 40 percent of the 30 million people 65 and older have incomes that are no more than double the poverty line. Even retirement winners can expect to lose some ground eventually from ebbing earning power, loss of pension benefits when a spouse dies, chronic illness and dwindling purchasing power due to inflation.

In 1991, the maximum Social Security benefit for someone retiring at age 65 was $1,022 a month or $12,264 a year—hardly enough to support even a modest lifestyle. And at a 5 percent rate of inflation it will take $2,650 in 20 years to equal the purchasing power of $1,000 today. When you consider the combined effect of interest and taxes, Treasury bills and other interest-bearing investments probably won't provide the growth you need.

With increasing health costs over the past decade (more than doubled) and elevated drug prices (the cost of drugs increased 152 percent), additional unplanned financial demands will be made on diminishing incomes and purchasing power. More than 85 percent of all people 65 and over take at least one prescription drug regularly.

Financial myths say that you will not need as much money during retirement as you do now. Not true! You will have more expenses for travel, leisure activities, hobbies etc. You can also plan on increasing medical expenses. Generally the average income from Social Security will not be adequate to the needs of the recipient. Medicare pays less than half of a retiree's medical bills. Many employers are cutting back on medical coverage for retirees because of costs.

In the face of these negative facts, what can aging people do to live better? Part of the answer is to make your voice heard by lawmakers to terminate punitive restrictions on income by persons who work while receiving Social Security benefits. Many people will elect to work until 70 and beyond. Older, experienced people are finding employment for their specialized skills.

Instead of thinking about retirement as a period of inactivity, think instead of it as an opportunity to discover new career ideas.

Consumption Of Time

One view of life is that it is all about consuming time in ways that we individually define as creative and joyful. How you view life is the driving force behind work, hobbies, organizational activities, and sports.

Organize your life so that you always have more things to do than there is time available to do them. Always have a project that you must do.

Instead of "Retiring" either keep working for financial gain or move on to work for psychic rewards. Because if you are not active consuming time can become a daily burden.

Work

A recent U. S. Department of Labor study on Workforce 2000 indicates that with the current focus by business and industry on work redesign to include the use of advanced technology, a skilled and literate workforce is required. This means that over 35 million Americans will have to improve their abilities and learn new skills in order to meet these labor requirements.

With our educational system in disrepair, one solution to this skills gap can come from the Third Age population which is better qualified to take on new, difficult challenges than younger people are. Younger entrants into the labor force between now and the year 2000 are declining rapidly. Those aged 25 to 34 will decline by 14 percent, while those 35 to 44 will decline 14.6 percent. Those over 45 will increase significantly.

As a result of these statistics, companies are planning to attract and retain productive older workers in the Third Age population to meet the challenge of a tight market for skilled and dependable labor.

With recent legislation eliminating mandatory retirement many progressive organizations desire to hire seniors. That is because of their proven ability to learn to operate sophisticated computer software, pay more attention to customer needs, have a lower turnover rate, fewer on-the-job accidents, and are rarely tardy or absent. Also their life experience equips them to interact, at all age levels, with coworkers in a most productive way.

Detailed studies commissioned by the Commonwealth Fund (as part of its Americans Over 55 Work Program) demonstrate the value of older workers to businesses worldwide. This report should encourage business to look toward capable, committed older Americans to fill many of the openings that will occur.

The report showed that older workers:

1. Can be trained to handle new technologies (including sophisticated computers and software) as quickly as younger staff.

2. Are just as flexible about hours and duties as younger workers—and in some cases even

more so.

3. Regularly establish much lower turnover and absenteeism rates than their younger colleagues.

4. Are often better sales people than younger staff members.

Data for the studies were collected from Days Inns of America, Inc., The Travelers Corporation, and B&Q plc, the United Kingdom's biggest chain of do-it-yourself stores. Among the revelations in the report was the fact that from 1.1 to 1.9 million men and women ages 50 to 64 are unemployed or discouraged, but are willing, able and well qualified to work. They want to work for financial reasons but the desire to increase their overall life satisfaction was rated almost as important as income.

To attract and retain older workers progressive companies are using:

1. Aggressive and creative recruiting to reach the Third Age population.

2. Flex time including part-time, flexible hours, job sharing, and growth career tracks.

3. Supervisory training on how to manage older workers.

McDonald's Corporation is aggressively recruiting older workers. It calls them non-traditional and is making a special effort to provide a hospitable working environment. It is using sensitivity training including videotapes featuring seniors describing their work experiences. Older workers are viewed as candidates for upward mobility.

San Diego-based Great American First Savings Banks has expanded its recruitment efforts to encourage older workers to apply for entry level jobs. Georgia Power is using retired customers with technical experience to help low-income seniors weatherize their homes.

Kelly Services, the nation's largest staffing support company, has a national Kelly Encore program offered to seniors in 850 locations nationwide. Starting in 1987, Kelly Services was the first staffing support company to recognize the special skills and experience that mature employees can contribute to the workforce. The Kelly Encore program provides seniors with the flexibility of mixing work and leisure at their own pace, thus providing the best of both worlds.

The Kelly Encore program includes: software training to update and refresh employee's skills. The computer training is user friendly, and self-paced which encourages the individual to learn at her/his own pace. Reference Guides are provided which detail the most frequently used software functions. Kelly also staffs a toll free hotline for employees to call when they have a software question.

Among the job options open to older employees through Kelly are: office services (accounting, clerical, data entry, receptionist, secretarial, typing, records management, switchboard); marketing (trade shows, comparison and performance shopping, merchandising, auditing, telemarketing); light industrial (warehouses, food service industries, production, assembly, electronic circuitry, maintenance, food preparation, and housekeeping); and technical (engineering, manufacturing, data processing, science, accounting, art and publication).

Seniors can work as homemakers, home health aides or live-ins, and assist individual clients with day-to-day activities like cooking, light housekeeping or personal care through Kelly Assisted Living Services, a subsidiary of Kelly Services.

Because of the flexible nature of the Kelly Encore program, mature employees are able to control the number of hours they work and the amount of money they earn without jeopardizing any Social Security benefits. Jobs are open to persons of all ages including those over 70 receiving Social Security without the earning limitations of those 65 to 69 years old.

There are many advantages that fit the lifestyles of most mature persons. Flexible work schedules, the opportunity to meet people and make new friends, enhancement of current skills and learning new ones through training programs.

It is a great way to maintain your financial independence with more than 100 work categories to choose from. Pay is based on the skills used on assignment and rates are increased as new skills are learned. Vacation pay, holiday pay and special bonuses are earned as well.

For more information contact Charlotte Schwartz, Vice President of the Kelly Encore Program, Kelly Temporaries, 1020 S. W. Taylor, Suite 240, Portland, OR 97205, (503)227-3850.

Among companies which hire older persons is Kentucky Fried Chicken which has made a commitment to hire older workers. Another is Teledyne Continental Motors which provides employees who are age 58 or older with 30 or more years of service, a number of special benefits. They include increased vacation time and improved insurance, pension and surviving spousal benefits.

Polaroid allows a rehearsal for retirement which provides an unpaid leave for up to six months. Approximately half of the employees who try this return to full-time employment.

Minnesota Title Financial Corporation uses a job-sharing method to provide options for continued employment.

At Control Data Corporation older workers are viewed as a vital resource and are aggressively retrained when technological changes make jobs obsolete.

The Travelers Companies based in Hartford, Connecticut use a retiree job bank program as an in-house temporary agency. The program has been so successful that Travelers recruited retirees from other companies to fill the demand.

The American Association of Retired Persons (AARP) has launched an employment planning and job search program called AARP Works. It is a series of eight job search workshops. Sessions include topics such as self-assessment, identification of skills and values, setting priorities, increasing self-esteem, job networking and interviewing skills.

As the concept of going back to work

becomes more widespread, people will soon adapt to the idea of successive careers. We will find ourselves cycling in and out of several different jobs throughout our lives. Each one will be interspersed with periods of rest, recreation, retraining, and personal reflection. And some older men and women will hit their career stride for the first time at an age when others are retiring.

Actually only 27 percent of Americans want to stop working completely at retirement age and more than 60 percent hope to keep working either full or part time. Changing attitudes and financial necessities will raise this percentage even higher. Retraining will become a normal part of work for everyone.

The health of older workers will continue to improve. More and more jobs are based on knowledge, experience and judgement and only a few on gross physical capabilities. These decreased physical demands mean not only that more older Americans are able to continue working but that more desire to do so.

In the near future, a fleet of wisdom workers will emerge. Mature men and women who will be retained and whose compensation will be based not on hours but on their experience, contacts, life experience, and wisdom. Retirement will not remain as it has been for much longer. And since most older people would enjoy a chance to continue working but in a more flexible, less pressured fashion, the key to redefining retirement will lie in restructuring the way we work and how we are allowed to interweave work and nonwork throughout our adult years.

The Institute of Gerontology at the University of Michigan turned up 369 variations of work and leisure in industry today. And with the explosion of telecommuting (computers at home linked to remote business offices) many people will work out of their homes.

With the aging of America, one area to look for work is to become a money management professional i.e., stockbroker, mutual fund sales person, financial planner, etc. Also, health related jobs will boom covering the full spectrum of job titles.

Among progressive companies that recognize the aging changes in the workplace are two outstanding ones. Metlife, with 43,000 employees, has a trend-setting program launched in 1992, Healthy Aging, designed to reach maturing employees company-wide with 10 wellness campaigns in areas like exercise, diet, and care giving.

Herman Miller, with 5,900 employees has redefined work, especially offering more part-time and flex-time employment in order to retain productive long-time employees. Nearly half of the company's workers are now 31 to 40 years old, and management expects to be prepared when that group moves into their 50s and 60s. The company's rehabilitation team not only works to minimize worker disabilities and injuries but channels its knowledge into new office furniture systems.

The company has produced an 18-page research summary, "Aging Workers In The Office."

It is chock-full of information about human factors, sensory changes in aging, and other findings relevant to office design. It is available at no cost by writing to Aging Workers, c/o Howard Johnson, Director, Personnel Services, Herman Miller, Inc., 8550 Byron Road, Zeeland, MI 49464.

Retirement, study after study is showing is not what the majority of Americans really want. Nearly half of nonworking adults report they would have preferred to go on working full-time when they stopped working. Those who stopped working involuntarily say they are less satisfied with their lives than those who chose either to continue to work or to retire.

Older workers believe—a myth—that they have to retire to make room for the young. Actually, we are running out of young people as their numbers entering the labor force go down. Another myth holds that Americans over 50 who have stopped working are happy retirees who enjoy traveling, spending time with grandchildren, and engaging in hobbies that earlier had been crowded out of busy parenting and working schedules.

The facts are that many older persons retire unwillingly from their jobs. The majority of men ages 55 to 64 indicate that they desire to continue working even if they have no economic need to do so.

The Law And Aging

The law is now positioned against ageism. No longer is there mandatory retirement. No longer can you be asked ageist questions during a job interview. No one can ask about:

1. Date of birth.

2. How do you feel about working with younger people?

3. Why are you coming back to work after so many years?

4. Do you have any handicaps?

The following questions may be interpreted as discriminatory by applicants who are not selected for the job:

Dates of school attendance.

Age of applicant.

Requiring that applicant submit a photograph before hiring.

Types of Work

The French christened it "Le Troisieme Age" the Third Age, the life beyond the job, after the First Age of growing up and the Second Age of working and/or parenting. As we approach the 21st Century that Third Age can last 20 to 30 more healthy, active years. It can be a time for a new style of living, working, and earning that no one could or should call retirement.

There are five types of work. Wage work, fee work, home work, study work, and volunteer work. A balanced work portfolio ideally comprises all five types of work because each provides distinct benefits. Now is the time, by using these five types of work, for the Third Age population to lead the way, to change the language, to set the fashion, and to show others that opportunities, not only problems, abound in the third segment of life.

Never consider volunteer work as less than worthy. In her book, *You Can Make A Difference,* Marlene Wilson says that volunteering does have a decided effect on a person's psychological and emotional well-being. But even more exciting, there is now sound research proving that volunteering prolongs life expectancy and improves the physical well-being of older persons as well. This was shown in the March 1988 issue of American Health Magazine in an article by Eileen Rockefeller Growald and Allen Luks, entitled "The Immunity of Samaritans: Beyond Self." They pointed out that epidemiologist James House and his colleagues at the University of Michigan's Survey Research Center studied 2,700 older people in Tecumseh, Michigan. For more than a decade they examined how social relationships affected the health of the subjects and concluded that helping other people results in real physical and psychological benefits.

In their article Growald and Luks reported that the Michigan study clearly demonstrated that doing regular volunteer work, more than any other activity, dramatically increased life expectancy. The difference was especially significant for men. It was noted that "Men who did no volunteer work were two-and-one-half times as likely to die during the study as men who volunteered at least once a week."

The authors also referred to other similar studies being done at Yale, the University of California, Johns Hopkins University, The National Institutes of Mental Health and Ohio State

University. These studies all seem to indicate that doing good for others through volunteering is not only beneficial to a person's nervous system but to the immune system as well.

The article concluded: "Just as people now exercise and watch their diets to protect their health, they may soon scrape peeling paint from their elderly neighbor's house, collect money for the March of Dimes, campaign for a nuclear freeze, teach illiterates how to read or clean up trash from public parks—all for the same self-protective reason."

Older Worker Studies

According to information in a study paid for by The Commonwealth Fund, Harkness House, One East 75th Street, New York, NY 10021-2692, (215)535-0400, the idea that older workers are not efficient was dispelled. Case studies at two large American corporations and a major British firm show that older workers are productive, cost-effective employees. The studies provide the first detailed economic evidence that older workers can be trained in new technologies, are flexible about work assignments and schedules, have lower turnover and absenteeism than their younger colleagues, and are often better sales people.

The studies were made at Days Inns of American, Inc., operating a nationwide hotel computerized reservations system; The Travelers Corporation, one of the world's largest multi-line financial services companies, and B&Q plc.

Days Inns began hiring older workers (50

and over) as reservations agents in 1986.

Travelers established a job bank of its own retirees at its headquarters in Hartford, Connecticut in 1981 which it later expanded to include non-Travelers retirees. The arrangement saves the company nearly $900,000 a year. In-house temps are highly productive because they know the company in a way that strangers cannot.

B&Q plc staffed a pilot store completely with workers aged 59 and over in October 1989.

As a result of their experiences with older employees the companies discovered that it made good sense to hire seniors.

The Commonwealth Fund, which underwrote the studies, has an "Americans Over 55" Program that started in December 1988 with the fundamental premise that people over 55 are an under-utilized resource with a tremendous productive potential. The program aims to:

Increase opportunities for continued employment of older American who want to work; motivate employers to find new ways to attract, retrain, motivate, reward, and retain seniors; and help educational institutions get into the business of providing continuous education and training of seniors who want to improve the value of their skills.

It's almost everyone's dream: working at a job or career one truly loves.

Innovative older people are following that dream into later life by switching to occupations that give them a sense of freedom, let them be their own bosses, keep them challenged, and allow them to help others.

Caroline Bird of Second Careers analyzed the career switches of 6,347 people over the age of 50 and the nearly 300 occupations they chose. The older workers today are pioneers, according to Bird. The work-minded seniors of the 1990s are testing out new work-styles. They are retiring the factory whistle that used to blow for all in favor of flexible jobs that give people new ways to fit work into their changing lives.

Rethinking work involves reevaluating every aspect of our lives. It causes us to look at our real sources of fulfillment.

Each year, the Labor Department creates thousands of part-time jobs for older persons through its Senior Community Service Employment Program. The employees work at senior centers, schools and hospitals. For information call (202)523-3871.

Computer Network For Seniors

Computer literacy is almost compulsory today if you have any interest in part time or full time work. Also, computer versatility is useful on the management of your own hobbies and financial affairs and enables you to relate to younger members of your own family who are probably all computer whizzes.

One organization is dedicated to helping seniors learn about computers. Its goal is "Bringing wisdom to the Information Age." This organization is SeniorNet, 399 Arguello Boulevard, San Francisco, CA 94118 (415)750-5030.

The company runs an online computer service that links you to other seniors who are learning and using computers as well as to a network of computer training centers. Training centers currently exist in locations throughout the United States.

SeniorNet has a low cost trial fee for its network ($9.95 per month). Usually the first month is free and the company will provide a free modem for those who need one. A modem is the device that allows information to be communicated between computers using regular phone lines.

SeniorNet's goal is to empower older adults to use computer technologies to encourage them to contribute their wisdom to the information age. Seniors are excellent workers and having computer skills makes us all more employable.

When Third Age members take on new interests they actually have longer life spans than those who are content with what they have already learned.

Laws

The Federal Age Discrimination in Employment Act (ADEA) is based on the fact that ability, not age, should determine an individual's qualifications for getting and keeping a job. Congress enacted the ADEA in 1967 to prohibit discrimination against older persons on the job and to combat prejudices about older workers. In 1978 Congress raised the protected age to 70 and in 1986 abolished mandatory retirement entirely except for a few specific categories of employees.

It is unlawful for firms with 20 or more employees to fire, refuse to hire, or otherwise discriminate against any individual (age 40 and above) with respect to compensation, terms, conditions, or privileges of employment. Forty four state laws cover employers with fewer than 20 employees.

The purposes of the ADEA are:

To promote the employment of older persons based on ability rather than age.

To prohibit arbitrary age discrimination in employment, and to help employers and workers find ways to resolve problems arising from an aging work force.

The law has transformed the work-place by:

Ending mandatory retirement in government and the private sector, except for limited categories of employees.

Striking terms such as "recent college graduates" or "age 20 to 35" from help-wanted ads.

Ending blatantly discriminatory employment practices.

Raising employers' sensitivity to age discrimination.

Another goal of the Act is to improve the monitoring of employee job performance. Older employees can still be fired for poor performance, but courts require documentation. The Act also eliminated retaliation against any individual for complaining about age discrimination or for helping the government investigate an age discrimination charge. Also covered are labor organizations, employment agencies and the Federal Government.

It is illegal to deny employees promotions

or training opportunities because of age, to reduce employees' wages or compensation based on age and for an employer to consider age when deciding whom to demote or promote.

Among other prohibitions in the Act are these: Employers many not target older employees during involuntary layoffs or reductions-in-force, or fire individuals based on their age. Employers are responsible for ensuring that managers and other employees do not harass older workers.

ADEA generally prohibits mandatory retirement at any age. Another piece of legislation, the Older Worker's Benefit Protection Act, prohibits discrimination in existing employee benefit plans after April 15, 1991.

Individuals protected by the ADEA cannot be denied the opportunity to participate in an employer's benefit plans because of age. It is lawful, however, for some employment benefit plans to provide lower benefits to older workers than to younger workers.

The American Association Of Retired Persons (AARP) has a Worker Equity Initiative with goals that include: combatting age discrimination in employment, assisting employers in recruiting, managing, training and retraining an aging, increasingly diverse work force, helping empower people to make informed employment and retirement decisions, advocating enforcement of nondiscriminatory rules, policies, and practices related to age in the work-place and developing innovative programs and models that will increase the older worker's options.

AARP also maintains the National Older Worker Information System (NOWIS), a computerized employer-to-employer data base that describes more than 180 innovative older-worker employment programs now in place in private sector companies. These are programs that promote full-time and part-time opportunities, job redesign, effective transition to retirement, and job retraining.

Management expert Peter Drucker has stated that one of the most significant opportunities for corporate innovation will be available to those companies that react early to changing demographics and make the best use of the tremendous resource older workers represent.

Indeed, how effectively we as a nation use this valuable resource will determine our productivity and global competitiveness in the 1990's and in the 21st Century as well.

Social
Security

On August 14, 1935, the Social Security Act was signed laying the corner stone for the most successful social program in American history. Thirty years later, on July 30, 1965 the Medicare program was established, adding health protection to income security for seniors. No other programs are more essential to the security of American families.

As the number of retirees increase, the government's ability to continue to provide for the large and growing population has become strained and as a result the Social Security benefit stream is under constant attack. The National Committee to Preserve Social Security and Medicare is a monitoring lobby group that is fighting to preserve and expand senior benefits. Their agenda includes defending present benefits and working toward building better ones.

The current issues are the inclusion of coverage of both long-term home health care and nursing home care, elimination of the earnings test, and correction of the Notch—reduced Social Security benefits for the more than 12,000,000 workers born between 1917 and 1926.

In the fiscal 1992 budget, President Bush wanted to reduce Medicare spending by $13.8 billion dollars. Hospitals were asked to absorb 66 percent of this cut. One major area affected would be payments to teaching hospitals which could result in a shortage of primary care doctors or specialists.

Hospitals continue to lose money on Medicare patients with rural hospitals being hit hard by the administration's proposed cuts. Medicare patients comprise 70 to 80 percent of rural hospital patients.

The current treatment by the Social Security system doesn't account for the equal role that women play in ensuring the economic well-being of American families. Women have lower average wages and their careers are often interrupted by family duties. Thus, they receive lower benefits as workers than as spouses. In effect, many are in the same financial position in retirement that they would be in if they had never worked.

When women drop out of the work force to care for children or aged parents they cut their future benefits since Social Security is based on the individual's highest 35 earning years. At the end of 1990 the average Social Security benefit for retired women was only 76 percent of that for retired men.

The obvious need is to give women credit for care-giving years spent out of the paid labor force.

Pensions

Money is an enabler not an end in itself. It is necessary to acquire enough of it to maintain the life style you desire and is necessary as a basis of your self image.

Your retirement income is at risk.

No one expected so many of you to live so long when they made all of those great promises about retirement and health care. This includes the federal government.

Now as bureaucrats face the new realities and recognize what it is going to cost, they are rapidly trying to figure out ways to avoid the obligations of the past. And due to legal loopholes, reckless investments, corporate raiders gobbling up pension assets or just an unsettled economy—the golden years may not be as secure as we have been led to believe. It's an unfortunate truth that many of us cannot depend on pension payments to supplement Social Security in our Third Age.

It is also a fact that only 39 percent of full-time private wage and salary workers aged 16 and over are covered by a traditional pension plan.

Even though Congress created the Pension Benefit Guaranty Corporation (PBGC) to protect the potential recipients of pensions of more than 40,000,000 workers, many lose benefits. This happens through bankruptcy or through annuities which their pension plans purchased from life insurance companies which may go bankrupt. Three to four million pensioners fall into this group whose benefits are no longer insured by the PBGC.

By paying monthly premiums to the PBGC businesses protect their workers pension benefits up to $2,250 per month. Recently concern has been expressed about the long term financial viability of the PBGC.

James B. Lockhart, executive director of the Pension Benefit Guaranty Corp., wrote an article for the *Washington Post* about the serious problem the PBGC faces. The article included the facts about back-to-back termination losses of $1 billion, a $2.5 billion deficit and an estimated growth in that deficit to more than $18 billion by the end of 1997 from under-funded pension plans.

Although, overall the defined-benefit

pension system insured by the the PBGC is healthy, with $1.3 trillion in assets to back up some $700 billion in benefit liabilities, the insurer faces an exposure of $40 billion in under-funded plans $13 billion of which is a near-term possibility.

Lynn Martin, U.S. Secretary of Labor said "PBGC remains vulnerable to substantial losses. Steps must be taken now to make sure the pension promises made to American workers are kept and American taxpayers are not faced with having to foot the bill for pension promises made but not kept by corporations."

One proposed solution is to have the corporate sponsors of well funded plans, which represent more than 80 percent of the plans, pay higher premiums. Since the defined-benefit pensions system is voluntary, the risk exists that responsible corporate sponsors will be driven out of the pension system, which is the lifeblood of American savings. The 1 million workers in under funded plans who have benefits in excess of the insured levels are also endangered. Change is needed now to prevent a pension crisis. Only 30 percent of pensions were guaranteed by the government in 1988, down from 39 percent in 1975.

Thousands of companies have replaced their traditional pensions with insurance annuities, removing them from the safety of the Federal Pension Benefit Guaranty Corporation.

Many other pensions are dependent on the success of company stock as the basis of their future income stream. With the frequency with which companies are getting into trouble it is doubtful if this represents a reliable source. More than half the traditional pension plans in the United States allow companies to withhold from pensions the moneies they have contributed over the years to Social Security.

In 1984 the Reagan administration gave it's blessings to corporations which wanted to terminate plans, where pensions plans contained more money than they were obligated to pay out, and to pocket the excess money. In 1990 employers terminated 11,800 defined benefit plans, the most common type. Fewer than one in ten pension plans offer a cost-of-living adjustment and along with longer life comes the increasing negative impact of inflation.

A study by Northwestern National Life Insurance Company, entitled "Retirement at Risk" shows how much health care will cost in retirement. These are costs not covered by Medicare and Medigap.

Present Age	Average Annual Health Costs At Retirement	Age When Your Money Will Run Out
25	9,652	75
35	8,132	80
45	6,521	89
55	4,878	90
65	3,360	+90

Average out-of-pocket annual health-care costs if you need home nursing care.

Present Age	And You Are Sicker At Age 70	Age When Money For Home Health Care Will Run Out
25	18,432	71
35	15,883	72
45	13,472	73
55	10,701	74
65	7,840	78

Roughly four in ten workers work for employers which offer health-benefits to retirees. But soaring health costs have companies cutting future retiree benefits. The six without employer-provided health care coverage who will have to bear the cost themselves, face soaring costs beyond that provided by Medicare and Medigap insurance policies.

About 32 percent of all employers offer health benefits to retirees, covering 36 percent of people older than 65 and 41 percent of those younger than 65.

The Families USA Foundation, a non-profit research coalition based in Washington, D.C. commissioned a report to see how much of their own money people, 65 and above, are spending on health care costs not covered by insurance or Medicare. Even after inflation was factored in, the study found that they spent more than twice as much on out-of-pocket costs in 1991 than they did before the federal government established Medicare. In 1961 the amount was $1,589 per family. By 1991 it had reached $3,305 or 17.1 percent of their after-tax income. And this does not include the taxes they pay to support government health programs.

These increases come when most people cannot afford them because they are at an age where their income is going down. A new accounting rule requires that corporations switch their accounting methods by 1993. The rule requires that corporations must deal with the health-care benefits as soon as the employee qualifies for the benefit. Now they are allowed to handle retiree benefits on a pay-as-you-go basis. When the retiree health benefit is paid it is reflected on the company's balance sheet.

This increased liability for future retiree health-care costs will speed up the trend of making new retirees pay a larger share of their costs. The cost is enormous for companies that have or will soon have a large population of retirees. Companies can write the new charges off all at once over twenty years. Chrysler Corporation faces a charge of $4 billion to $6 billion. GM, with a retiree population of 350,000 will take a non-cash charge against earnings of $16 billion to $24 billion to reflect benefits already promised to the automaker's employees.

This new regulation will accelerate the trend to limit retiree health care benefits. The parade of Standard 106 changes is building. The dominant trend is to set a maximum annual amount on what the company will pay for each retiree's care.

IBM for example will cap payments at $7,000 per year.

The message is loud and clear. If you want a secure retirement, then you better start planning for it, and paying for it yourself.

Where will your retirement income come from? Men of 65 are expected to live another fifteen years and women another nineteen years on the average. However as we all move to healthier life styles we will fool them all and live much longer.

As the number of seniors increases government will renege on its psychological contract with the U. S. population regarding retirement income and reduce benefits to retirees by postponement and limitation.

At five percent inflation to preserve $1,000 of today's purchasing power you need an income stream that provides $1,280 in five years, $1,620 in 10 years, $2,080 in 15 years, and $2,650 in 20 years.

What should you do?

Do not retire. If you are retired go back to work. Most company-based health care programs reimburse a major portion of prescription costs. If you are working and your employer offers an HMO option, by all means take it.

If you are retired sign up for a Medicare HMO. An HMO, for a small monthly fee, and a small charge per medical visit, will take care of all your medical costs.

Use your political power to ensure that the Federal Government does something about the health care crisis and provides adequate protection so that both corporate pensions and health care commitments are protected against the profit motive.

Security in the Third Age now has to rest with each individual of the 120 million-member U.S. labor force.

Heart
Disease

The definitive book setting new directions for avoiding heart disease is Dr. Dean Ornish's program for *Reversing Heart Disease* (catalog).

The program he writes about combines eating a low-fat, low-cholesterol diet, getting regular exercise and avoiding stress, resulting in a single comprehensive system to prevent, halt, even reverse coronary disease without drugs or surgery.

This book includes scientific proof that:

Greater reductions in cholesterol levels than have ever been reported without using drugs resulted as a direct benefit of Ornish's program.

After only one year the majority (82 percent) of program participants had demonstrated some measurable average reversal of their coronary artery blockages. Even a small amount of reversal causes a relatively large improvement in blood flow to the heart.

Many participants in the program "were able to reduce their medications or eventually discontinue them altogether under the supervision of their physicians."

Physically, the program can help to open your heart's arteries and you feel stronger and more energetic, freer of pain. Emotionally, it can help you to open your heart to others and to experience greater happiness, intimacy, and love in your relationships. Spiritually, it can help you open your heart to a higher force and to rediscover your inner sources of peace and joy.

In its news bulletin, the AARP review said of the program: "People who were oldest and had the worst arteriosclerosis improved the most."

Diet
And
Aging

In the May 1992 issue of the Reader's Digest an article was published entitled "The Look Younger Diet" by William M. Hendryl. It reported on the work of Dr. Kenneth Cooper, president and founder of the Aerobic Center in Dallas, and of Jefferey Blumberg, associate director of the U.S. Department of Agriculture's Human Nutrition Research Center on Aging at Tufts University in Boston.

Both agree that research shows that many so-called age related declines in physiological function seem to have less to do with aging than with environmental factors like diet and exercise. They report that obesity is one of the leading causes of accelerated aging. Cooper says, "If you lose weight, stop smoking and exercise you can slow the aging process and make dramatic changes in your looks in a relatively short period of time."

Blumberg adds, "There's certainly a link between good nutrition, a positive attitude and improved quality of life. People can have a say in what's going on with their bodies by selecting a healthful diet." Blumberg also recommends drinking six to eight glasses of water or other fluids each day to help keep skin and other tissues hydrated. "That's especially important for older people who are at risk for dehydration because their thirst drive becomes blunted with age."

Good general nutrition, says Blumberg, is essential to maintaining a healthy, youthful appearance. And the key to good general nutrition is balance. The scientist admits that while we all have a lot to learn, indications are that by paying closer attention to nutrition we can slow the effects of aging.

The May 1992 issue of the Nutrition Action Health Letter published by the Center For Science In The Public Interest has an exciting report on Nutrition and Aging. Bonnie Liebman interviewed four of the researchers at the U.S. Department of Agriculture's Human Nutrition Research Center On Aging at Tufts University. The center was established in 1977.

Here is what the researchers reported:

A number of elderly people who may be

written off as victims of Alzheimer's or senile dementia, or suffer neurological symptoms, such as stinging or abnormal gait can be brought back to normalcy by the proper nutrition analysis and an injected vitamin supplement.

Older people are deficient in certain vitamins because of a change in the absorption or utilization of the vitamins. There are some dangers from overdoses of certain vitamins.

Older bones have different nutrient needs than younger bones, and evidence is accumulating that shows cataracts and muscular degeneration can be delayed with proper nutritional supplements. Certain nutrients can enhance the immune system.

The bottom line is that Michael F. Jacobson, Ph. D. executive director of the Center for Science in the Public Interest, in an editorial said, "I believe there is now sufficient evidence to warrant people taking supplements, some at many times the USRDA, on top of an excellent diet.

Our bodies have a set point (like a thermostat) that defends the weight it is set at. It does this by slowing down metabolism when a person is losing weight and holding it low when he returns to normal eating until the weight reassumes the set point which the body protects.

Dieting trains the body to become a more efficient energy machine. As a result, persistent dieters find themselves pushing a stone up a hill that gets steeper every time they push.

In addition, since all prior generations suffered to some degree with not enough to eat, we are programmed by history that eating well means success.

The ability to turn excess food energy into fat is a biological heritage shaped by the experience of all prior generations. Few were the ancestors who did not have to contend with an annual rhythm of scarcity and plenty. When a hungry season ends, people do not merely resume their average rate of food consumption, but instead indulge in ritual bouts of overeating. Feast follows fast. Anthropological evidence suggests that the hunter gatherer population never got fat because of their mobility. They were more likely to suffer temporary food shortages, but less likely to suffer from prolonged starvation. It was also true that fat reserves in these people were drawn down several times a year by temporary scarcities of some animals and harvestable wild plants. In addition, the amount of walking, running, digging, and carrying they had to do would have burned up most of the extra calories they consumed when food was plentiful.

Exercise physiology demonstrates that in today's world the key to resetting ones set point downward is running. The body responds to the message that running gives and keeps you slim so that you can be a more effective hunter. That's the survival signal that is built into our bodies by our heritage.

We must recognize that weight control is a never-ending, lifelong battle against great odds. However, the food industry is awakening to the demand for healthier food. Never before has there been the proliferation of fat free and cholesterol free foods. Foods many of us have given up on. Bread, cheese, sour cream, cake, cookies, ice cream, and yogurt, and the low fat products follow along.

We cannot deny the facts. Food can be the enemy. We alone can befriend food and make it an ally in the pursuit of healthy aging.

Strength
Training

If somebody promised you that within three months you could be stronger than you've ever been, fit-looking, full of zest for living, brimming with enthusiasm and in possession of a body that felt young, confident and vigorous, would you believe it?

The fact is you can remarkably improve your body in 90 days even if you are an octogenarian and in the process develop increased muscle mass that will protect your bones, increase your resistance to fatigue, improve your mental faculties and put more oomph in your sex life.

What's the catch?

There is none, unless you absolutely refuse to engage in a simple program of strength training that will renew your body and give you an awakened sense of passion and control over your life that may have been missing for a long time.

Information provided in the June 1992 issue of Nutrition Action News Letter published by the Center for Science in the Public Interest quoting research from Tufts University, makes clear that the single most important step to reversal of the aging process is strength training.

By preserving and increasing your muscle mass you can prevent the appearance of the classic signs of aging which are an accumulation of a lifetime of inactivity. The solution is high intensity weight lifting. People aged 65 and older can be made stronger than they've ever been in their lives. A 90 year old can be made stronger than a 50 year old. Muscle strength can be tripled in older people.

Thigh muscles are a prime target of improvement in older people because the object is to prevent falls. On a long term basis the goal is to strengthen legs, back muscles, and upper body-arm and chest muscles. The Framingham Heart Study showed that half of women aged 65 can't lift ten pounds. Women have less muscle mass to begin with, and they start to lose muscle strength more rapidly after 60. They can become so profoundly weak that they have to be institutionalized. They become victims of the idea that fragility is a natural outcome of growing old. It isn't! Fragility occurs because muscles are neglected. High intensity weight lifting can restore resiliency to muscles, make them grow longer and add mass that protects bones. High-intensity weight-lifting means lifting a weight heavy enough that the lifter will be fatigued after eight or nine lifts. If you lift a weight 15 times, it is too light. It won't increase strength.

Gyms that work with older people on strength training start them out at about 60 to 80 percent of their maximum lifting capacity. For nursing home patients, that's about five to ten pounds. In a healthy 65-year-old doing knee exercises, it's about 20 pounds.

Weight lifting may promote weight-loss as well. The number of calories burned at rest is determined by muscle mass. So the more muscle mass you build, the more calories you burn. Strength training can be done inexpensively. You can fill up a one-gallon milk container with water for an 8.3 pound weight. You can buy big rubber bands in a sporting goods store to tie to a chair to do resistance exercises.

As you will see, aerobic exercises are also an important part of good health for older people. Researchers at Tufts University state that if they had to choose only one type of exercise to recommend for older people it would be strength training. That's because it has more to do with everyday functional activities. Muscle weakness goes up rapidly after age 70. At age 20, 90 percent of the volume of the thigh is muscle. At age 90, it's only 30 percent muscle. That's one reason the biggest risk to older women is from falling down. With weight-lifting you can increase muscle mass

10 percent, but the increase in strength is 200 percent.

A good weight training program is designed to prolong vitality by retarding or even reversing the usual biological deterioration process that people past 45 often begin to experience. Such things as the slowing down of metabolism, glucose intolerance, and declining strength can be reversed and the benefits of weight training act to postpone disability by reducing the risk of such chronic conditions as heart disease, Type II diabetes, arteriovascular disease, hypertension, and osteoporosis. Overall, weight training prevents the development of a common old-age malady called "sarcopenia" (lack of use).

Long-term studies bear out the fact that the average person's lean-body mass declines with age. These studies show that Americans tend to lose about 6.6 pounds of lean-body mass each decade of life. The rate of loss accelerates after age 45. Two things are responsible for how much muscle we have. The first involves how much we use our muscles. The second is the level of tissue-maintaining anabolic hormones circulating in our blood.

How much a muscle is used is partially responsible for its size and lifting capability. Used frequently, a muscle will maintain the status quo. A muscle that is not only used frequently but is pushed to the limits of its capacity will grow and gain strength, even in elderly people. The second muscle-size factor is the amount of anabolic hormones in the bloodstream. Anabolic hormones increase the synthesis of protein. The most potent of these is testosterone. Because men have much more testosterone in their bodies than women, they also have more muscle. Studies have shown that vigorous exercise can cause a phenomenon called "muscle hypertrophy" meaning individual muscle cells grow larger. The same studies offer pretty conclusive evidence that muscle mass and strength can be regained, no matter what your age and no matter what the state of your body's musculature before you start your exercise program.

For many of you muscular conditioning is an alien concept. Once you get started you will find that as your muscles grow bigger and stronger you will be able to substitute heavier and heavier weights. The strength-building program has two objectives: (1) the muscles of your upper body—those in your arms and shoulders; and (2) the muscles in your hips and legs—your lower body.

Upper-Body Conditioning exercises include:
      The easy push-up (or Bent-Knee Push-Up)
      Arm Curl (or Biceps Curl)
      Chest (and Shoulder) Exercise
      Upper-Arm (Triceps) Exercise

Lower-Body Muscular Conditioning exercises include:
      Knee Extension (and Flexion)
      Hip and Knee Extension
      Step-Ups or Stool Stepping

It is strongly recommended that you keep a

log book as a motivational tool. You have to recognize that it will take four to six weeks before the benefits of increased strength and energy become apparent. You can expect to encounter some muscle soreness. It appears to be the way our muscles adapt to exercise training. It's completely natural. As your strength increases you can decide to either continue to have your muscles grow or move into a maintenance mode. In the maintenance mode you should continue training three days a week.

Two strength training researchers have published encouraging information on muscle building by older persons. William Evans, PH.D., and Irwin H. Rosenberg, M.D., of Tufts University's USDA Human Nutrition Research Center on Aging, Boston, Mass. (301)556-3000 wrote a significant book in 1991 entitled *Biomarkers* (catalog). In it they reported dramatic new evidence on what makes the body decline, pointing out that it is not the passing of years but, to a great extent, the combined effects of inactivity, poor nutrition and illness, much of which can be modified. They found that no group in our population can benefit more from exercise than senior citizens. They conclude that much of the loss of muscle as we age is preventable and even reversible at any age. Proof of this were the results of strength training for two separate groups:

A 12-week program of strength training using 60 and 70 year-old-men resulted not only in substantial increases in strength (their lifting ability went from 44 to 85 pounds), but also in muscles that were larger and leaner with less fat in and around them. The strength of their quadriceps more than doubled and the strength of their hamstrings tripled. The average daily increase in the extensors was 3.3 percent and the flexors 6.5 percent. The research conclusion was that the amount of muscle growth for this older population was as much as could be expected from young people doing the same amount of exercise.

An eight-week study (Figure 3) of 87 to 96 year-old-women showed that resistance exercise tripled their muscle strength and increased muscle size by 10 percent. Experience with the old-old-group, (the frail elderly) showed an increase of strength by as much as 180 percent and muscle mass by up to 12 percent by following a program of resistance exercise. This population's quality of life and ability to walk soared.

Older people may be slower to respond to exhortations about exercise, but when they finally do it they are more committed than the typical young adults. Older people tend to circle around the idea of exercise for a while before they commit themselves.

You have to recognize that you have to break the habit of non-exercising. Behavioral psychologists tell us that it takes 21 days to establish a pattern and 100 days to make it automatic. You should make a minimum commitment for that length of time when starting this major change from inactivity to activity.

The primary goal of weight training is to keep people independent through exercise. There is

FIGURE 3: BUILDING STRENGTH IN THE FRAIL ELDERLY

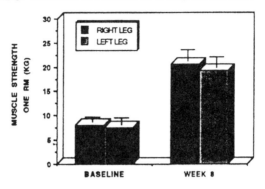

An eight-week study by Dr. Maria Fiatarone shows that the frail, institutionalized elderly can build strength through exercise, too. Her subjects were 10 men and women—aged 87 to 96—from a midsize chronic-care hospital. Her premise was that the quality of life of the "old old" can be improved by making them stronger, more capable of getting around by themselves, and less prone to falling.

Dr. Fiatarone focused on the relationship between her subjects' leg muscle strength and their ability to walk. She found the stronger they were, the faster they could walk a 20-foot course.

The graph shows how much the subjects' leg strength improved over the course of the study. Leg muscle strength almost tripled and the size of their thigh muscles increased by more than 10 percent. Perhaps as important was the psychological effect. The subjects confidence in their ability to walk—and walk faster than they had only eight weeks earlier—soared.

Printed with permission from *Biomarkers*, Copyright 1991, Simon & Schuster.

Independent confirmation of the value of strength training comes from Pat O'Shea, professor emeritus of exercise and sports science at Oregon State University. He wants to keep elderly people out of nursing homes with a prescription of barbells and leg lifts He proposes a major change to traditional exercise programs for older people that focuses exclusively on aerobic workouts. His idea is to reach people in their 50s and set them on a weight-lifting course that can last into their 80s and beyond.

The benefits of the weight training O'Shea expounds range from the improvement of overall strength to positive self image. If your thighs, hips and abdominal are strong, you're less likely to lose your balance or fall. Your range of motion improves with weight training, And weight training reduces body fat while increasing lean-body tissue. While his program includes aerobic workouts, he believes weak muscles, not a weak heart, often rob the elderly of their independence.

"People don't go to nursing homes because they are cardiovascularly unfit," he says. "They go there because they lack the strength to lead a functional home life. It doesn't do much good to have a strong heart if you lack the strength to get out of a chair, or you can't get from your car to the supermarket."

O'Shea says a weight program doesn't threaten high blood pressure because it focuses on major muscle groups, the thighs, hips, low back and abdominals—and high repetitions that encourage muscle endurance, rather than the bulking up from low repetitions with heavy weights. The overall exercise plan O'Shea recommends sends you to the weight room two to four times weekly. Fewer workouts aren't beneficial and too many workouts court injuries. Choose six to eight exercises that work different parts of the body—for instance, bench presses for chest and hip and leg presses for quadriceps and do eight to 12 repetitions.

As with any new exercise, you should begin with easy workouts and gradually increase weights. Training is easier with friends, and O'Shea advocates lifters find two or three training partners. Training partners also can provide the most important support: the impetus to keep going. Once a person starts feeling well he'll keep going.

Exercise

The capability to run long distances, which is the human biological heritage is still evidenced today by native peoples who are athletically fitter than most Americans. The Tarahumara Indians of northern Mexico hunt deer by chasing them for as long as two days. They keep them constantly on the move. The Indian chases the deer until the creature falls from exhaustion. It is then throttled by the man.

Among the Nganasan in Siberia, hunters can overtake a young wild reindeer and seize it by the leg after chasing it for 10 kilometers. The Ache of Paraguay still use the run-down method to hunt deer, and the Agra of the Philippines run down wild pigs.

Until recent times heavy exertion was built into the lifestyle of most people. Even the bookkeeper of the nineteenth century chopped wood to heat the house and the workplace. Today, however, only six to eight percent of our population exercises adequately to preserve their vitality throughout their lifetimes. But what is the direct benefit of regular exercise? Individuals who exercise regularly enjoy better functional capacity. You may live longer, too, but more importantly you may live more years independently and postpone or entirely eliminate the need for institutional care. (See Figure 4)

Exercise is the central ingredient of good health. It tones the muscles, strengthens the bones, makes the heart and lungs work better, and helps prevent constipation. It increases physical reserve and vitality. The increased reserve function helps you deal with crises. Exercise eases depression, aids sleep, and enhances every activity of daily life.

It is well proven that physically fit men die four times less often from cancer than do men who are not fit. Physically fit women die from cancer 16 times less often than unfit women, and men and women who are fit are eight times less likely to die from cardiovascular disease.

Regular exercise helps reduce blood pressure and levels of harmful LDL cholesterol, while increasing the beneficial HDL cholesterol. Men and women who are physically active into older age are less likely to develop osteoporosis, and physically fit women are 33 percent less likely to get diabetes than unfit women.

Impressive figures, pointing out that the benefits far outweigh the inconvenience.

You are never too old to begin an aerobic exercise program and to experience the often dramatic benefits. Always start slowly and build up slowly. Those who do too much too soon are the ones that get into trouble. You should be able to carry on a conversation while you are exercising. On the other hand, you should be breaking sweat during each exercise period if the exercise is performed at normal temperatures of approximately 70 degrees. The sweating indicates that the exercise has raised your internal temperature.

You need an exercise goal of 200 minutes per week spread over five to seven sessions; beyond this amount no further benefit seems to result.

Your choice of a particular aerobic activity depends on your own desires and your present level of fitness. The activity should be one that can be graded. That is, you should be able to easily and gradually increase the effort and the duration of the exercise.

What's the payoff for exercising regularly? The answer is marked improvement in the organs of your body and a demonstrable increase in physical well being. Among the changes are:

Brain—an improved sense of well being, less depression and anxiety.

Lungs—improved capacity to use oxygen

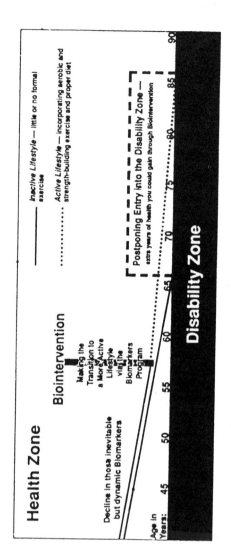

Figure 4

This figure demonstrates that by making a transition to a more active lifestyle incorporating aerobic and strength-building exercise and proper diet you are able to postpone chronic illness and disability.

Reprinted with permission from *Biomarkers*, copyright 1981 Simon and Schuster.

and increased strength and endurance of breathing muscles.

Heart—stronger, more efficient heart muscle, more blood pumped with each heartbeat and slower resting pulse; collateral circulation expanded.

Muscles—increased strength, improved energy storage, better blood supply, improved capacity to take in and use oxygen and increased mobility and flexibility.

Bone—maintains its strength (density) and delays development of osteoporosis.

Tendons and ligaments—increased flexibility.

Body composition—less body fat and more lean body mass.

Hormones—lower blood sugar level, and lower adrenaline at rest (which decreases anxiety and muscle tension).

Coordination—improved reaction time and better balance.

Blood—increased oxygen carrying capacity, more efficient body cooling, increased blood volume, higher HDL (good) cholesterol level and lower triglyceride level.

Exercise should be fun. Often it doesn't seem so at first, but after your exercise habits are well developed, you will wonder how you ever got along without them.

Aerobic exercise refers to the kind of fast-paced activity that makes you huff and puff. It's good for you. It places demand on your body's cardiovascular apparatus and, over time, produces beneficial changes in your respiratory and circulatory systems.

There are three parameters under your control, frequency, distance or duration, and speed or intensity. Speed should always be considered last.

Frequency refers to how often you exercise.

Duration is the length of time devoted to each exercise session.

Intensity is a measurement of the level of your exertion during each workout.

Inactive seniors should start with walking and then graduate to jogging, swimming and brisk walking as fits their individual desires. You always want to consult your doctor before starting an exercise program.

Develop exercise as a routine part of your day. For seniors, gentle activities performed daily are more beneficial and less likely to result in injury, particularly when getting started.

Many people will not want to exercise the 200 minutes a week. You can get most of the benefits with considerably less exercise. At 100 minutes per week you get almost 90 percent of the gain you get with 200 minutes. At 60 minutes per week you get 75 percent of the benefit you get with 200 minutes.

Part of the myth of aging is that ability declines with age. While this is true it is insignificant as Figure 5 will demonstrate.

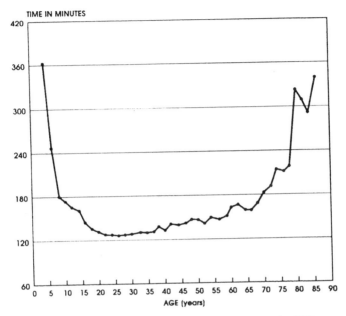

United States Marathon Age Records, 1986

Figure 5
Shows marathon records as a function of age. It does shows that older marathoners take longer but only compared to younger marathoners. When compared to the general public older marathoners outperform 90 percent of younger people at any age.

Printed with permission from *Aging Well,* by James F. Fries, copyright 1989 Addison-Wesley

Memory

Wе now know that while some forgetfulness is normal with advancing age, severe memory loss that disrupts your life is not normal. Often, the culprits turn out to be disease, over-medication or other disorders. Often, but not always, there is a cure.

Recent research suggests that short term memory, memory of specific recent events, is the type of memory most likely to decline with age. After age 50, it's normal to experience some loss of your short term memory, and by 80, just about everyone does. However, there are researchers who disagree that there is any age-related loss of short term memory.

The good news is that your short term memory can be enhanced through lifestyle changes and mental exercises. Keep ongoing lists. Flex your memory muscles. Challenge yourself daily with crossword puzzles and other word games. Taking a class and learning something new can stimulate your mind, your memory and your interest in life. An active life is crucial for an active memory.

Your long term memory, your lifetime accumulation of information and the memory that controls procedures such as driving a car or tying your shoe, does not decline. In fact, your long term memory actually improves with age.

Long term memory and its successful functioning has been divided into learning, retention and recall. Staying intellectually active maintains learning ability, but not too much is understood about retention. As a result, there is little the researchers can recommend at this time.

Indications are that the older we get, the longer it takes to recall facts. But recollection of facts is another skill that can be learned and kept sharp with some simple tricks. See the suggestions at the end of this section.

Normal aging does not inevitably make you fearful, forgetful and feeble-minded. Instead, most people's minds can stay almost as active, flexible and vital as in youth. And in some ways the mind gets even sharper. Because of the large store of experiences that accrue with age, late life can be the richest time for our minds.

There is no reason to expect a life-altering general mental decline as you grow older. Indeed, intelligence tests have shown that most people retain their mental prowess, and some even improve their intelligence scores with advancing age. Think of the mind as a muscle. It also needs exercise to continue to grow.

Walter M.Bortz II M.D. in his book *We Live Too Short And Die Too Long* (catalog) reports on a study done by K. Warner Schaie and Sherry Wallis of Penn State University in 1986 entitled "Can Decline in Adult Intellectual Functioning Be Reversed?"

According to Bortz, 229 subjects were studied who ranged in age from 64 to 95, with an average age of 73. The effects of lifestyle on mental functioning was very important. Half of the subjects showed no mental decline in a 14-year period between 1970 and 1984. Seventy-one subjects underwent five one-hour training sessions (in which a variety of mental chores were provided) and then were retested. Those individuals who declined in intellectual ability in the 14-year observation period responded more favorably to the training than did those who showed no change during the span of years. This indicated to the researchers that the longitudinal decline was reversible to some extent.

The upshot of the study was that there is continuing plasticity of behavior into adult life.

This means, the researchers said, that at least in a substantial portion of the community-dwelling elderly, observed cognitive decline is reversible. It is likely to be attributable to mental disuse. In other words, mental sharpeners, and memory could be manipulated and improved through relatively simple and inexpensive educational training techniques.

What the intervention procedures seemed to accomplish was to reactivate behavior and skills in the subject's behavioral repertory that had not been actively employed. Other studies on the intellectual activity of older persons show a direct correlation between exercise and improved mental functioning. Bortz showed in his book that Robert Dustman and his colleagues proved that exercise three hours a week for four months led to "clear improvement" in intelligence. Theodore Bashore of the Medical College of Pennsylvania extended these studies with the same finding.

A 1988 report from Ontario cited studies in which fit older subjects tested higher in intelligence tests than did sedentary control subjects. And a study from the Netherlands recorded that the recall capabilities of 40 nursing-home patients (average age 83) improved after an exercise program.

You can do a lot to keep memory sharp at any age. As the research shows, stimulation by learning adds to your brain power. Learning is like any skill, you have to practice it. Older people take longer to learn things. What the older person lacks in speed he or she makes up in experience and wisdom.

We need to be as mentally active as possible; engaged, not isolated from interesting and challenging ideas. Such findings encourage us to break from routine and take on a difficult mental task such as a new, challenging game like bridge or chess; a new subject such as history, computers, math, languages or new ways to do daily work.

Giving the brain a daily workout is just as important as exercising your muscles. The result, if the brain is kept active, can be what was once called the wisdom of old age. The younger chess player may think faster; the older player has learned to think better.

Staying
Aware

In order to be informed consumers of medical services you have to work at it. The authors have discovered that while they have access to superb medical professionals, they find that practitioners are reactive rather than proactive. Frequently it is necessary for us to aggressively request information on a particular new medicine or an early detection examination in order to have the test made. We suggest that you subscribe to a group of medical newsletters:

The Harvard Heart Letter, P.O. Box 420234 Palm Coast, Florida 32142-0234, (800)829-9171.

The John Hopkins Medical Letter, "Health After 50," P.O. Box 420179, Palm Coast, Florida 32142.

Harvard Health Letter, P.O. Box 420300, Palm Coast, Florida 32142-0300.

These letters are informative and will keep you abreast of new technology, medications, advances and tests available for early detection and prevention of disease.

As the rate of innovation accelerates the value of these letters, giving impartial evaluations, increases.

The Senses

The five senses vision, touch, hearing, smell and taste tend to lose their sharpness with age. They decline at different rates and different degrees for aged persons. The age of onset and the rate of decline differ markedly among people since variability goes up with age. Some of us, however, experience no sensory decline.

Disease and environmental factors influence deterioration of the sensory organs. Intense and prolonged noise affects hearing; smoking often reduces taste and smell sensitivity and accidents may injure the eyes.

These losses can be significantly compensated for by the existing and growing availability of assistive devices. Before now the aging myth and the lack of knowledge of availability has inhibited their use. As an example, people are reluctant to use bifocal glasses because they are supposed to be a visible indication of their age. Failure to take advantage of assistive devices can mean reduced mobility, increased dependence on others, lessened ability to communicate, frustrations, difficulty in accomplishing tasks and not feeling good about oneself.

Vision

The majority of older adults have good to adequate vision but several aspects of vision do change with age. These changes include decreased visual acuity (sharpness), farsightedness, changes in color perception, decreased sensitivity to light, and decreased ability to adapt to glare. If we practice preventative care and seek prompt treatment most of us will go through life with nothing more harrowing to contend with than a pair of bifocals.

For bifocal wearers who work on video display terminals and personal computers special glasses which are designed for ergonomically sound body position and optimum viewing of the screen and copy are recommended.

Hearing

Hearing loss is potentially the more serious of the sensory impairments. Unlike poor vision, hearing loss rarely inspires sympathetic understanding.

In the high frequencies hearing loss begins soon after birth and continues throughout life. Although a hearing aid often enhances social participation many older persons find hearing aids annoying, because not only is the sound of the human voice increased, but all sounds are amplified. Some of the newer digital based hearing aids can solve this problem. The news for those with severe hearing problems is promising as scientists apply the latest in electronic miniaturization to this problem.

Taste

Food that tastes and smells good is important in maintaining a good level of nutrition. However with increasing age the senses of taste and smell decline and can affect the pleasure and satisfaction older people obtain from food. These changes usually do not seriously affect taste sensitivity until the seventh decade of life.

Smell

Many older people have difficulty identifying common foods and environmental substances by smell. Because of the importance of attaching a name to an odor, expanding smell and taste vocabularies is one way to increase enjoyment of the sense we've got. Wine tasters and perfumers can distinguish fine gradations of taste and odor because they've trained themselves to do it and because they've developed a vocabulary to work with. The recommendation is to think about what you're smelling, and work to find words to describe it.

Touch

Although research is limited, studies suggest an age-related decline in the sensory system of touch. Simply by paying more attention to the sense of feeling will your fingers seem more sensitive.

See *Aging Well* by Thomas Hager and Lauren Kessler (Catalog.)

Incontinence

R emember your first *accident*—the panic, the feeling of the loss of control, the inner scream "I'm getting *old.*" Loss of bladder control has happened to thousands of men and women and despite reliable methods to cure the problem, many people still believe little can be done about it. This is not true, but unfortunately, newspapers, magazines and TV have added to the confusion about incontinence by intimidating you with announcements that you must accept bladder problems as a condition of growing older. Nonsense! The majority of persons who have experienced incontinence can cure it. You don't have to become an older member of the diaper set. Incontinence is not only avoidable for the most part, but largely reversible.

Here are the facts: One out of 25 Americans, or almost 10 million people have difficulty controlling their bladders. While 85 percent of incontinence problems occur with women, until recently there was no medical specialization in urology focused on women's problems. Women's problems were addressed by nurses. A program to increase professional awareness of incontinence was spearheaded by Dr. Katherine F. Jeter in 1984, the founder of Help For Incontinent People. Treatment is now popularly available as a result and the health care field is moving to the point that every hospital and health maintenance organization will have a "urological advisor."

Bladder disorders present an enormous challenge to both the people who have them and the doctors and other health-care professionals who treat them. Bladder problems are enmeshed in a complex web of negative social attitudes that makes talking about them painful, even to our closest relatives or friends, and makes asking for help difficult if not impossible for many. People who have these problems often suffer intensely from guilt and shame, which may prevent them from seeking the help they so desperately need. Even some doctors are uncomfortable talking about bladder disorders, especially urinary incontinence.

Even though this problem is easy to treat,

studies show that only one out of twelve people consults his doctor or nurse for help. Adult diaper commercials discourage rather than encourage people to look for appropriate treatment. In addition, in the past many people have been told by their physician that nothing could be done to help them.

The medical phrase for uncontrolled loss of urine is urinary incontinence. Incontinence can affect people of all ages, but is especially common in women and men over age 65. As a woman ages, her uterus and pelvic floor sags, changing the angle at which the urethra exits the body, predisposing the leakage of urine. In men, benign enlargement of the prostate gland tends to block passage of urine from the bladder until the bladder overflows. Drugs such as diuretics can cause major surges in urine flow. Tranquilizers, anticholinergics, anti-depressants and other drugs can block the normal voiding mechanisms, resulting in retention of urine and then incontinence. Always suspect that the drugs you are taking might be aggravating the problem.

There are several types of incontinence:

1. Stress incontinence, (physical stress) in which urine leaks in response to a cough, sneeze, laugh, or other sudden movement;

2. Urge incontinence, in which you feel an urge to urinate but may not have time to get to the toilet;

3. Reflex incontinence, a variation of urge incontinence in which you urinate suddenly without any warning;

4. Overflow incontinence, in which the bladder over fills and leaks without any warning and without any feeling.

5. Mixed incontinence, in which several types of incontinence are present at the same time. About one third of women who have stress incontinence also have urge incontinence as a result of a hyperactive bladder. Older men often have urge incontinence coupled with overflow incontinence which occurs because of prostate enlargement.

Bladder control problems should *never* be considered as a natural part of growing old, something you have to put up with. Incontinence is *not* an irreversible part of aging. Don't believe anyone who tries to convince you that it is. Actually, there is usually a good chance that your bladder control problem can be cured or greatly improved. You can and should do something about it.

Becoming incontinent can disrupt your life. You may become afraid to leave your home, or stop seeing your friends and family, and even your sex life may not be the same. But by not dealing with the problem directly, millions of people miss out on full, enjoyable, productive lives. For many, treatment can begin without the use of drugs or surgery. You might start by doing something simple, like changing some of the foods you eat or reducing the amount of caffeine and alcohol you drink. Your doctor also may want to change the dosage of certain medicines you take. You also can start a course of bladder training or pelvic muscle exercises. For most people incontinence can be improved and managed in a way that will help them resume or preserve their normal lifestyle. Proof of this was reported by the National Institute for Aging which, in cooperation with the Alliance for Aging Research, recently presented the results of a new study which showed that bladder training can help reduce or eliminate incontinence in many women over 65. Men also can benefit from this kind of treatment.

Bladder training is a simple program that does not use drugs or surgery. The patient goes through a six-week course with a doctor or nurse, in which education is provided about the bladder, and the patient learns to keep a strict schedule for using the toilet. Patients also are taught how to relax or distract themselves if they need to go to the bathroom before the scheduled time.

The program is particularly good news for women because the loss of hormones after menopause and stress to the bladder caused by childbirth make them more prone to incontinence, doctors say. Depending on the cause and extent of the problem and on the individual woman's social and psychological circumstances, treatment may enable her to continue to work, to enjoy social activities, and to remain active.

The program may work for you if you experience the following problems:

You leak when you bend over, lift heavy objects, cough, or sneeze (stress incontinence), or you get a very strong urge to go the the bathroom but can't hold the urine long enough to get there in time (urge incontinence). If you have these kinds of problems, this program may be a good first step treatment for you and your doctor or nurse to discuss.

If your doctor or nurse does not think that bladder training will work for you, there are several other choices to think about, such as learning exercises to train the muscles that hold urine in, taking one of several medications, or in more serious cases, having an operation.

In March of 1992, the U. S. Department of Health and Human Services issued new guidelines for detecting and treating urinary incontinence. The guidelines, issued by a 15-member panel of experts and lay people, estimated that 10 million Americans are afflicted by urine control problems. The panel reported that 80 percent of those afflicted with the embarrassing and under-treated condition could be cured or greatly improved with proper therapy and called for doctors and other health workers to inquire more aggressively about possible problems of bladder control and to test to determine the underlying cause. The panel acknowledged that incontinence costs the nation more than $10 billion a year in health spending and lost productivity.

Among the techniques for bladder control recommended by the government panel is the one of double voiding. Here, you empty the bladder as much as you can, wait a minute or so, and then empty it again. It is surprising how much additional urine will sometimes be present.

For stress and urge incontinence, pelvic muscle exercises, called Kegel exercises, named after the doctor who popularized them, have the potential of restoring normal or near normal bladder function and are very appealing. Kegel exercises work on the sling-like group of muscles that stretch from the pubic bone in front to the tail bone in the rear. These muscles surround the anus, the urethra (the tube that drains the bladder) and, in women, the vagina. Squeezing them can cut off the flow when you go to the bathroom—much like putting a clamp on a garden hose.

These exercises strengthen the muscles that control the urinary outlet. Practice stopping urination in midstream and then starting again. This is often very difficult, especially for women, but the exercise will build sturdier sphincter muscles. To build strength in these muscles, contract the ones around your anus and urinary tract and hold for 10 seconds. Relax, then repeat the exercise. You will build strength in these muscles and help tighten the pelvic floor. Current recommendations suggest you perform the exercises for two minutes three times per day, which should equal at least 100 repetitions. Each contraction should be held 10 seconds or more to establish sufficient muscle strength.

Dr. J. Andrew Fantl and his colleagues at the Medical College of Virginia in Richmond have developed a bladder control program that is encouraging to women. At first the women who participated in the program were asked to relieve themselves at 30 to 60 minute intervals depending on how long they could comfortably wait. If urgency occurred, patients were taught to suppress the urge using relaxation and distraction techniques. Women kept daily treatment logs turning them in for evaluation during visits to the clinic weekly. As they showed improvements and were able to keep to their schedules they were asked to extend the waits by 30 minutes. The goal of the program was to reach a two and one half hour to three hour interval.

After the six week program the women were encouraged to follow the schedule most comfortable to them. Out of the 123 women, 15 gained complete continence and 92 improved by 50 percent or more. The program has been approved by the National Institute of Aging for widespread use.

Fantl says he believes that with proper treatment most women can show improvement or even be cured. The knowledge gained from his study will eventually show that incontinence treatment may actually prevent or delay a woman having to enter a nursing home.

For more information on this program and incontinence call the toll free number of the Alliance for Aging Research (800)237-4666.

You can purchase a Pelvic Training Manual and audio tape for $6 from Help for Incontinent People (HIP) Inc., P.O. Box 544, Union, SC 29379, (803)579-7900.

Another reference worth consulting is a book which you'll find in the catalog section of this book. Consult *Overcoming Bladder Disorders* (catalog), by Rebecca Chalder and Kristene Whitmore, for more details on how to identify and exercise the pelvic muscles and send for the HIP material as well.

You may need help in isolating the muscles that need to be exercised and doing the exercises correctly. It makes sense to consult your doctor and get the proper start and direction. Best of all when you consult him make him listen to you and be sure he hears what you say. Your doctor will probably perform a complete examination on you with emphasis on the abdomen, rectum and the urinary openings. A urinalysis usually will be performed. If there are abnormalities, cystoscopy (inspection of the inside of the bladder) may be indicated.

For women, the physician will sometimes prescribe a local estrogen cream, which can be surprisingly effective by softening the vaginal tissues, making them more elastic and capable of greater tightness.

In spite of a significant amount of research, the prostate is still something of a mystery. Each year more than one million men develop prostate disorders in three broad categories:

Prostatitis, which includes infection, inflammation and non-bacterial conditions;

Benign prostatic hyperplasia (BPH), non-malignant enlargement of the prostate gland; and

Prostate cancer.

Prostatitis means inflammation of the prostate. It can result with or without bacteria being present. Curative therapy consists of short or long term high dose antibiotic treatment which is not always successful. Suppressive therapy consists of long-term low-dose antibiotic therapy, which will sterilize your urine and likely relieve your symptoms, but will probably not prevent reinfection.

Between ages of forty and fifty, the prostate begins to enlarge, as glandular structures begin slowly to proliferate. By age fifty, noticeable symptoms occur in at least half of all men. Almost all men who survive into their eighties will have significant enlargement. Control of bladder overflow as a result of enlarged prostate can often be achieved through pelvic exercises. A new medication, Proscar, has been satisfactory, say physicians, in reducing prostate enlargement. For stubborn cases, surgery may be the alternative.

Late in June 1992 the FDA approved Proscar for shrinking enlarged prostate glands. The drug marketed by Merck Sharp and Dohme is expected to benefit 30 to 40 percent of men with benign prostatic hyperplasia (BPH) a non-cancerous condition that affects about half of men by the time they reach age 60.

Common symptoms of BPH include difficult and frequent urination. Clinical studies show the drug offers significant symptom relief for about one in three men, says Dr. John D. McConnell of University of Texas Southwestern Medical Center in Dallas. The drug can shrink prostate gland size by up to 20 percent. Side effects include about four percent of those treated who have reduced libido or difficulty getting an erection and can make diagnosing prostate cancer with the PSA test more difficult. Proscar cost $1.40 per day for as long as a man takes the drug.

The drug options mentioned work by

relaxing the prostate muscle to relieve pressure on the urethra or by eliminating the hormones that stimulate the prostate to grow. Of good news to older men in a new test referred to above, that is extremely accurate in very early detection of prostate cancer. It is called the PSA test which stands for prostate specific antigen and can identify prostate tumors before they can be felt by a doctor during a standard digital rectal exam. PSA is considered the most useful cancer marker yet discovered. This is particularly significant because prostate cancer is the most common serious cancer affecting men.

Obviously, it takes effort to do what is necessary to keep the prostate and the bladder under control—exercise and medication mainly—but it works and for men and women who want to stay young it is not a burdensome requirement.

Don't accept defeat, or the idea that aging is another word for decay. Embrace your powers!

Assisted
Living

Assisted living is a way to provide a better physical environment for elders, for example, with cooking facilities in a resident's own apartment that can be supplemented with provided meals when needed or desired. Its appeal to older consumers is that it allows them to maintain dignity and independence. At their best, well-planned programs offer residents a greater sense of contributing to and controlling their own lives. Assisted living is starting to break away from the umbrella of "retirement communities." The field is expected to boom in the 1990s, and it is essential that we all understand this new alternative and the legislative drives and philosophy behind its emergence.

Driving elder housing developments will be federal nursing home reforms that now eliminate reimbursement for intermediate-level facilities. The Omnibus Reconciliation Act (OBRA) of 1987 combined skilled and intermediate care facilities into one category that no longer includes some older persons who will need community alternatives.

The state of Florida recently enacted legislative changes to promote assisted living as a care option by skilled nursing facilities. As of January 1, 1992, the state extended its licensing capabilities to handle more extensive hands-on-care within assisted living communities, called Adult Congregate Living.

Oregon created an incentive program to encourage health and wellness among its Medicaid-qualified residents in assisted living. Goals are set for residents during their entrance assessment. If the goal is achieved within three months, the state pays the community an incentive bonus. Everybody gains, especially the resident, who becomes more active and less dependent.

This is the beginning of providing tax advantages for taking care of ourselves, in government certified programs that result in the reduction of health care costs. The Third Age population, by taking care of itself, is capable of solving the health care cost problems our country is facing.

The states are likely to embrace assisted living as a preventive-care alternative to nursing homes. Assisted living has the potential of emerging as a viable option for project developers, professional care-givers, referral sources and elders nationwide.

The how manys of the Third Age population and the resulting market they represent will evoke the best of capitalism and entrepreneurship which will profit from helping us to regain lost capability and then keeping us well.

Legislation enacted under OBRA 1990 now allows states to use Medicaid dollars to pay for services in assisted living units. It is expected that by the end of the 1990s assisted living programs will be as regulated as nursing home care is today. An estimated 1.5 million Americans now live in about 40,000 assisted living communities around the country, ranging from campuses housing a full range of services to complexes that mix and match services by contracting with local providers. The federal government will actively drive this program because assisted living costs are estimated to be 20 percent less than nursing facility expenses.

Services generally include three meals a day, help available for elders having difficulty in eating, bathing, dressing and grooming. Reminder services exist that advise when to take medications, provisions for 24-hour security, and programs to promote health and wellness.

Assistive
Devices

Our independence can be enhanced if we accept and use some of the 17,000 assistive devices available to help us overcome physical limitations and disabilities. The elderly are four to five times more likely to suffer activity limitations than those younger than 65 and yet they only utilize ten percent of the available rehabilitation services. We are all reluctant to use assistive devices because they are a visible stereotype of aging. We must learn to value these tools to preserve our mobility and independence and sense of control over our lives even as our functionality declines.

With the advent of Title III of the Americans with Disabilities Act effective January 26, 1992, business and industry have to provide equal access to all their facilities, products, services and jobs. This includes provision of auxiliary aids and services. Primary initial focus will be on auxiliary aids for hearing, speech, visual, and mobility impairments. Historically, the impaired and disabled have essentially been invisible because of both social stigma and restricted accessibility. Out of sight, out of mind.

Now these limitations will be blown away and we will all deal normally with the use of assistive devices to overcome limitations. More socially acceptable terms such as hearing impaired, visually impaired, and mobility impaired will come into usage replacing such negative labels as blind, crippled, deaf, handicapped, etc.

The Technology Related Assistance Act defines an assistive technology device as "any item, piece of equipment, or product system...that is used to increase, maintain, or improve functional capabilities of individuals with disabilities."

Examples are:

Communication devices for those with speech or hearing impairment.

Environmental control systems for those with limited mobility.

Adaptive computer systems (eg. voice recognition) for those with sensory or physical disabilities.

Alerting devices to ensure safety for those

with Alzheimer's disease.

The Technology Related Assistance Act sets aside federal funds to establish consumer responsive statewide programs that promote assistive technologies for persons with disabilities. The goal is to build independence with assistive technology. One of the objectives is to assist businesses in developing plans for workplace accommodations.

The U. S. Department of Education, National Institute on Disability and Rehabilitation Research (NIDRR) operates ABLEDATA, an extensive and dynamic database containing information on 17,000 assistive devices for persons with disabilities. The ABLEDATA facilities are housed at the fully accessible Silver Springs Center at 8455 Colesville Road, Silver Springs, MD 20910, in the offices of the National Rehabilitation Information Center (NARIC). The two complementary projects will provide a service to persons with disabilities and their families, administrators, educators, and others interested in using or acquiring assistive devices or rehabilitative information.

Through ABLEDATA, anyone can acquire information on assistive devices ranging from eating utensils to external building modifications. Queries are handled by phone (800)346-2742, mail, fax (301)587-1967, TDD, and in-person visits. Requested information is available in print, enlarged print, braille, on audio cassette, computer diskettes, tape, and CD-ROM. Additionally, computer owners can access the database by means of a modem and a thesaurus is available to facilitate searches. The program has an enlarged screen display and print options for persons with visual impairments. There is also a bilingual staff member available to handle inquires in Spanish.

Searches for information can result in any number of citations, which are listings of all the data that the database contains on a particular item. Fees for printed citations are 1 to 20 citations are free; 21 to 100 are $5.00. Any number over 100 citations are charged $10.00 and $5.00 for each additional 100 citations. ABLEDATA's main objectives are not limited to simply providing timely information on state-of-the-art assistive devices but also to acquire new product information from manufactures, and to continue to enhance professional and public awareness of the ABLEDATA system through proactive outreach programs and training.

A special fact sheet for Assistive Devices for People with Arthritis is available to make life easier. Devices can alleviate pain and stress on joints, conserve energy, and help maintain independence. The fact sheet includes a bibliography for additional information about aids for independent living.

In June 1992 3M announced a new style hearing aid which is different from those presently marketed because it is programmed to fit the user's exact hearing loss, by a computer in the hearing professional's office. It gives the hearing-impaired person up to 8 different settings to choose from, each one computer-designed for a specific listening situation is his life. Each setting is programmed to improve speech understanding and sound quality in different environments, such as a noisy restaurant, a sporting event, parties and work. According to 3M, it provides a quality of sound not available in other hearing aids and it doesn't have to go back to the factory every time it needs an adjustment.

Another advantage of the device is that if the listening environment changes in the user's life, or if the hearing loss changes, the 3M instrument can be quickly reprogrammed for the new situation. The 3M instrument is adjusted by easy-to-use controls right on the hearing aid. There are no remote controls, no tiny settings to read, no need to learn anything about computers or technology. All the user needs to know is what sounds good to him.

Prices are reported to range from $550 to $1,400 depending on individual needs. Call (800)882-3M3M.

There are 58 educational captioned film/video libraries strategically located nationwide. Application for loan services can be made to: Captioned Films for the Deaf, 5000 Park Street N., St. Petersburg, FL 33709. This is a service provided by the U.S. Department of Education.

General Motors offers a reimbursement of up to $1,000 to cover the cost of adaptive equipment installation on a newly purchased vehicle. Call Mobility Assistance Center (800)323-9935.

Chrysler Corporation allows a cash incentive up to $500 per vehicle for adaptive expense for up to two new vehicles. Call Physical-

Challenged Recourse Center (800)255-9877.

There are two large-type weeklies with national circulation. *The World At Large* is a new weekly tabloid-size large type news-magazine that presents news stories selected from and published simultaneously by *U.S. News and World Report, Time* and other magazines. It includes a large version of the *Los Angeles Times* Syndicate Sunday crossword puzzle. A one-year subscription is $65, a six-month subscription, $37. Order from the The World At Large, Dept. M, P.O. Box 190330, Brooklyn, NY 11219 (800)285-2743.

The New York Times Large Print-Weekly offers a comprehensive sampling of the week's top news and feature stories, as well as its famous crossword puzzle.

G.K. Hall & Co., 70 Lincoln Street, Boston, MA 02111 (800)343-2806 has a catalog of over 500 large print books that are the same size and weight of ordinary books.

Over 12 million people in the U.S. have a visual impairment that interferes with normal reading and writing.

Digital programmable hearing aids can reduce background noise and restore one's understanding of a conversation.

The rate of change in innovation to overcome natural limitations is going up. One must keep continually aware and be aggressive enough to take advantage of the solutions that are available as well as being reevaluated by the proper medical discipline on a periodic basis. New innovations as a result of the advance and miniaturization of computer devices will enhance social participation.

Airlines are responding with special assistance which includes boarding assistance, flight arrival assistance, checked wheelchair assistance, a TTY data communications function that allows hearing-impaired persons to make reservations using a teletypewriter and telephone hookup, special meals, oxygen when required for use during the flight, stretchers, braille emergency briefing cards. They also welcome seeing eye dogs.

The Virginia Geriatric Education Center at the Virginia Commonwealth University in cooperation with a wide range of cooperating organizations is putting on a series of live video conferences to train various professionals on how to participate in promoting the independence of older adults through the use of assistive devices. Researchers see that many chronic diseases tend to be clustered in old age and frequently cause losses of function.

A key principle of geriatric care is the maintenance and restoration of function. However many of those who treat the assistive needy focus on the disease rather than how we can function in spite of it. We must use our personal power to reject the myths that prevent us from using assistive devices. We must do whatever we can to preserve our functionality. Assistive devices can be categorized as low and high technology.

Low technology implies rather unsophisticated common-sense products. For example, lower work surfaces, products that support independence in walking, sitting, moving in bed, feeding, dressing, bathing, grooming, toileting, communicating and recreation.

High technology tools include computer assisted everything as well as closed circuit magnifiers for those with low vision.

In the following some of the assistive devices available are described as well as hints on what we can do for ourselves to remove restrictions that inhibit our full participation in society, work, love and life.

Glasses

Bifocal wearers who have to tilt their heads and risk sore necks working at computer terminals can overcome the drawback by having a special pair of glasses designed that are optimal for working at the distance to the screen and for reading copy to be typed from.

Reaching Devices

A reaching device is available for people who have difficulty reaching items on higher shelves. The device, with a pistol grip and spring loaded suction cups at its end, provides users with the ability to pick up cans and jars.

Walkers

For many people, a walker (a mobility aid that provides a portable base of support) can be the critical difference between watching and taking part. Individuals of all ages use walkers for balance, weak knees or ankles, arthritis, etc. The popular conception of a walker is a lift up and put down device that is cumbersome at best. What most people don't realize is there are dozens of types (rigid, folding, two-wheeled, four-wheeled) and options (handgrip, brakes, attachments).

One of the leading walkers is the Able Walker, used successfully by more than 55,000 people in the last five years. It was designed to help people who have difficulty moving around to regain independence and freedom. The chrome, lightweight, Able Walker has four wheels, and a shopping basket that converts to a seat for resting. It has adjustable handle bars that slide up and down to the desired height and can accommodate individuals from four feet, ten inches to six feet, six inches. The locking button brake controls on the foam-covered handlebars provide safety and stability when sitting. The walker can be folded and easily taken in a car.

The Able Walker has been reviewed favorably by the American Association of Retired Persons, doctors, occupational therapists, hospitals, rehabilitation centers, and nursing homes. It was named the best medical/dental invention in 1991 and was cited as one of 1990s best innovations by the *Los Angeles Times*. Contact Able Walker Canada, 16-2350 Beta Avenue, Burnaby, B.C. V5C 5M8 (604)299-3444 or Able Walker U.S.A., Building C-2, 1122 Fir Avenue, Blaine, WA 98230 (800)663-1305.

Able Walker

Hearing

U.S. Bank in Portland, Oregon has recently added the ability to communicate with TDDs (telephone devices for the deaf). The TDDs integrate keyboards and telephones to bypass the need for voice communication. The customers can type messages and receive typed replies by customer service representatives.

Microsoft Corp. has joined the ranks of companies such as WordPerfect Corp and Lotus Development with its roll out of a Telecommunications Device for the Deaf (TDD) service.

Low Vision

U.S. Bank has added specially designed checks for the visually impaired with embossed lines and a larger size making it easy to locate the writing space for the date, payee, amount and signature.

Remember, devices don't make people independent; it's the use of them that does. It is not enough to provide devices. Education and motivation to use them has to be provided also.

To encourage the development of assistive devices the American Society on Aging has an annual Design Competition and awards that are given at its annual meeting. The primary sponsor of the design competition, now in its fourth year, is the Whirlpool Appliance Group of the Whirlpool Corporation. In March 1992 the First place award went to Xerox/Kurzweil Personal Reader. The device, with models that cost from $7,300 to $11,950 depending on add-ons, uses a portable optical scanner that converts almost any printed or typewritten text into spoken language, by the use of artificial intelligence and intelligent character recognition. The device gives persons without eyesight the freedom to read whatever they want, whenever and wherever they want.

While blind or vision-impaired persons of all ages are using the readers, they are especially useful to older persons with sight affected by strokes, diabetes, macular degeneration, glaucoma and other conditions associated with aging. Manufactured in Peabody, MA, the machine is compatible with software for word processing, communications, screen review and Braille conversion. For information call (800)343-0311.

Second prize went to Fiskars, Inc., for its Softtouch spring-action scissors, designed to be comfortably used by elders whose dexterity is limited because of weak hands. (715)842-2091.

Honorable mentions were given to:

Ariens Company of Brillion, WI for its lightweight, easily maneuverable Metro Snow Thrower, designed to greatly reduce the amount of physical exertion required for snow removal.

The Love Lift Co., Holland, MI was cited for its prototype of a portable home lift that allows for the safe transfer for a frail elder, for example from a bed to a wheelchair.

First Alert Smoke and Fire Detector for its light test on fire detectors. It eliminates the need for dangerous climbing on a chair or ladder to push a button. Instead one passes a flashlight beam across the test button to see that the device is working properly.

Awards were also made to students for the designs of a one-piece syringe for self administration of insulin for sight impaired persons, a chair to enable a person with little upper-body strength to shift weight more safely and easily while trying to stand, a line of women's clothing designed especially for older women, and a universal vacuum cleaner which is simple to use and easy to operate.

Disability
and
Aging

The American with Disabilities Act, which became effective January 26, 1992 mandates that individuals with disabilities be given the opportunity to participate in or benefit from any goods, services, facilities, privileges, or advantages provided by public accommodation. These goods and services must be provided on an equal basis.

No qualified job applicant can be denied employment because of a disability. The Act guarantees equal opportunity for individuals with disabilities in public accommodations, employment, transportation, state and local government services, and telecommunications.

A public accommodation must provide auxiliary aids and services when they are necessary to ensure effective communication with individuals with hearing, vision, or speech impairments. Since disabilities affect 22 percent of older women this will open up significant opportunities for enhancement of their lifestyles. But even more significantly because the disabled will become visible in the mainstream, the use of any of the 17,000 assistive devices that are available will be accepted more commonly without any negative stigma.

Aging does not mean disability or inability. However, as we age we are more susceptible to a variety of disabling conditions. With the technology advancing in all areas of the health sciences and the new visibility of the disabled assistive devices being used we become more functional and less disadvantaged. No longer need the disabled be hidden from public view nor be denied the social cultural pursuits they can enjoy.

We may not have become a kinder, gentler culture, but we have become more tolerant and because of this tolerance more freedom is afforded us all.

Do not accept or equate disability with non-activity, the two expressions are not synonymous.

You may not know that the new American Disability Act now requires employers to hire people despite handicaps. Now the handicapped have to learn how to job hunt and a new book has emerged to help them. It is entitled *Job Strategies for People with Disabilities* by Melanie Astaire Witt (catalog).

The book will help you:

Uncover your marketable skills step-by-step. Help you write standout resumes and go through successful interviews and show you how to make the job you want fit you.

Heretofore, work has often been denied to the one fifth of American adults who have disabilities. The book recommends that disabled persons develop a positive attitude, come to terms with their disabilities and, despite their limitations, lead a satisfying life.

When a disabled person applies for a job, he must be able, with or without reasonable accommodation, to perform the essential functions of the position. Reasonable accommodation is a modification or adjustment to a job or work environment. There are three types of preemployment accommodations.

Type one ensures equal opportunity in the application process. A prospective employer may make a reader available, for example, to read employment forms to an applicant who has low vision.

Type two ensures that on-job reasonable accommodations are available to enable employees with disabilities to perform the essential functions of the job. An employer may modify a work schedule, provide an amplified telephone handset, or reassign nonessential tasks to other workers. It would be considered reasonable in most circumstances for an employer to raise a desk on wooden blocks for an employee who uses a wheelchair or allow an employee who is blind to bring a guide dog to work.

The disabled employee must be given the opportunity to pay the portion of the accommodations that constitutes undue hardship to the operation of the employer's business. Type three ensures that on-job reasonable accommodations are required to enable employees with disabilities to enjoy benefits and privileges of employment that are equal to those which are enjoyed by employees without disability. An employer may have to make the employees lounge physically accessible.

Commenting on the ADA the chairman of the President's Committee on Employment of People with Disabilities, Justin Dart said, "ADA holds the potential for the emancipation and productive independence of every person with a disability on earth."

Cofounder of the American Coalition of Citizens with Disabilities, Dr. Frederick A Fay, who faces each day with multiple disabilities, quadriplegia complicated by a neurologic disorder says: "It doesn't matter whether you walk on wheels, talk with your hands and hear with your eyes, see with your ears, or communicate with the world with a computer keyboard and modem as I do. What matters is that you consciously keep a contemporary self-portrait in your mind of what you want and what you can do in the world of work."

We must adjust our thinking about special

needs. Those with special needs are entitled to public support. Special needs can be anything to anyone who is lacking, in any degree, full functionality or mobility in any area of daily life. Legislation has provided the tolerance, by law, of disabled persons, and funds made available to provide tools and assistive devices to them.

These rights for the disabled provided by law are subsidized by your taxes and should be utilized as fully as all other rights we are guaranteed.

Mature Driving

According to the American Automobile Association in its publication "Straight Talk For Older Drivers," by the year 2020, 50 million Americans will be 65 or older and at least 90 percent of them will be licensed to drive. This growing population of older drivers demands attention. Drivers can learn to compensate for the physical effects of aging. Mature drivers can improve odds of avoiding accidents by changing driving techniques, improving physical condition and choosing a vehicle that meets their special needs. Understanding the needs of older drivers can improve driving for everyone.

Effects of aging vary from person to person, but few older drivers have reflexes as sharp as those of a 25 year old. Older drivers, however, have one great advantage: experience. The longer you drive, the more you learn about what to do and what not to do on the road. What you lack in quick reflexes, you can make up in sound judgment.

According to research findings, exercise is the best way to fight fatigue, depression and loss of mobility at any age. Exercise can slow the aging process and improve driving skills.

Careful selection of driving routes can also improve performance on the highway. Older drivers should choose routes that provide ample lighting, well-marked streets, easy to read road signs and easy to reach parking places. Many communities offer driver improvement courses for people over age 50.

Federal and state regulators are struggling with how to deal with identifying older drivers who pose a hazard while not discriminating against those who don't. The number of motorists older than 65 has doubled during the last 20 years. And while older people, as a group, have a smaller rate of fatal accidents than teen-agers, their fatal accident rates based on miles driven are among the highest. Scientific research also suggest that reflexes and cognitive skills critical to driving deteriorate markedly after age 75.

In 1990, about 22 million of the 167 million licensed drivers in the U.S., or 13 percent, were older than 65. The number of older people driving will grow markedly in the years ahead, with the fastest growing group being those older than 85.

In a 1988 report on aging drivers by the National Research Council an arm of the National Academy of Science, found that while there was no basis to restrict driving on the basis of age alone, drivers 75 or older are twice as likely to be involved in accidents based on miles driven.

Signs on some highways, like the New York State Thruway, are being enlarged or made more reflective so older motorists can see them better at night. This is because most signs are designed to be visible at 50 feet, a standard too difficult for the eyesight of 40 percent of all drivers 65 to 74, the National Research Council report found.

At least a dozen states have laws requiring more frequent physical examination, road tests or license renewals for older motorists. However the trend is away from restrictions based on age. The prevailing thinking by researchers and regulators is that one's ability, not age, should determine who can drive. Officials in some states are experimenting with restricted licenses. This idea seems to have broad support because limited licenses will allow people to drive longer but avoid some of the hazards of unlimited licenses.

Medications
Side Effects

E arly diagnosis and treatment can eliminate many of the illnesses associated with aging. However, the Third Age individual must be aggressive with physicians. You must not take ill-informed medical options as gospel. You know yourself better than anyone. Never let a doctor convince you against your better judgement that you are ailing as a result of aging infirmities. Ask for second and third opinions. Rely on your own sense of your rightness about yourself.

Stand by your own opinion. Never accept as a medical condemnation so-called infirmities as the only options you have.

Depression is another "shrug the shoulder" attitude. No one seems to take into consideration that the person past 65 is more liable and susceptible to side effects from medication.

Drug company trials to qualify for FDA approval of a new drug are tested on a small number of people (typically three to five thousand) and when the drug is used on a large population, particularly older people, many more side effects can and do occur.

Medication will have an impact on you. You may have been taking a prescription for years but suddenly you start to have symptoms which you don't relate to the medication nor does the doctor. For example, a medication which you are taking causes a side effect that is diagnosed as xyz. You are given a medication to counteract the symptoms caused by xyz. That medication causes severe depression. You go to the doctor and say, "I am very depressed." The doctor says it only natural, after all you are getting on in years. Don't accept this easy solution. Accept the fact that the medication *may* be the cause. Ask the drug company. Ask your pharmacist what are the possible drug interactions or side effects. Do not accept anyone's explanation when you think there might be another answer.

Depression, sleeplessness, irritability, tenseness, GI problems are not the norm. Any and all of the above can be caused by reaction to new drugs or a reduced tolerance to prescribed medications.

Before you accept any of the above symptoms as "normal" examine every medication you are taking. If you don't have access to the Physicians Desk Reference or one of the popular consumer prescription guides, ask the doctor or pharmacist to review the potential side effects with you and the interaction of one drug with another as a cause.

The infirmities of age are often a creation of people who don't have the time, energy, or concern to delve deeply into what the real problems are. Depression is one of the very common side effects of medication in the 65 and over group. You may have built up an intolerance and do not know it. Depression is a destroyer of relationships and self esteem. If you are feeling depressed seek a physiological reason before accepting it with the shrugging attitude that the cause is aging.

Late Bloomers
And Your
Inner World

We all have the ability to be creative. It is not something that is unique to the great and visibly gifted, or the young. The secret of blooming, at any age, is related to how we feel about ourselves—how we affirm our self-esteem, how we hang on to feelings of personal worth and our sense of competence. Our self esteem is what ageism and the myths of aging attack the most aggressively and destructively.

This is the major reason we must reject the myths for ourselves and work to change our society so that our children and their children will not be subjected to these negative forces. We are happiest when we are utilizing all of our native capabilities. When we are using ourselves up. That's what life can be all about. It's why retiring from an active life has such a negative impact on many people whose sense of worth is identified with their work.

We must always fight to preserve our sense of worth and our sense of control over the events of our lives. Our self esteem is always under attack as we age.

Often people, relieved of the pressures of younger years, and with a hard won sense of self worth, can be more creative in their later years and discover talents they never dreamed they had. Creativity is the expression of the human spirit—to be studied, cultivated and cherished and rewarded with recognition. The ultimate incentive for each individual is the creative experience and the ongoing satisfaction that comes from fulfillment. (Not to be confused with productivity.)

Creativity does not always result in a product. The creative experience can result from introspection and a change of attitude. Our association with others, can be instructive and productive. This too is creativity. Rededication to earlier ideas and spirituality is a creative experience. The definition is yours and it is not limited to the artistic or to a product, other than love and satisfaction.

Each person defines the creative experience uniquely. It is whatever is meaningful to the individual involved. Even failure has positive payoffs. We can sometimes learn more from failure than from success if we do not allow ourselves to be defeated. The creative person affirms life and takes risks with joy and high expectations. Creativity can be the aging individual's most profound response to the limits and uncertainties of existence. Creative activity can become as consistent and dependable as any other personality characteristic, and more rewarding.

The sheer joy and being-aliveness in creative activity has its own way of triumphing over the inroads of debilitation and the unrelenting movement of time. All of our life experience can contribute to launching us into creativity. Every age, within the parameters of life experience, provides its own special opportunities for growth. To be truly fulfilled you want to reexperience the feelings of those moments in life you would most like to relive in order to recapture the sensations. This is a place we would like to be most of the time.

There are two roads to high. The first is the false road. It uses sensory saturation, liquor, and drugs to induce an artificial high. Its negative side effects are the perpetuation of infantilism, the lack of real commitment to other people, a poor self image, sickness and early death.

Most will choose the preferred, more difficult, but ultimately more rewarding route of exploring our own creative potential. It results in natural highs with positive side effects such as healthy self-image and the ability to live comfortably with whatever inadequacies that have kept you down before. You can be creative. Don't be afraid to take risks. There are two times in our lives we can comfortably be at risk. That is when we are young and before we take on the heavy load of family responsibilities and again in the Third Age when we have discharged those obligations and are free to rediscover ourselves.

Life is about having enough money and self esteem and a focus on creativity. If you learn how to manage them you are on the road towards your own outer limits.

It is unfortunate that 70 to 80 percent of the people you deal with have strong feelings of inadequacy. This is a result of "I'm not okay" feelings left over from childhood. In the intense getting and spending times of our middle years when we are making our way in society figuring out who we are and what is this thing called marriage and child rearing, we have little time for ourselves. In the Third Age we have time to revisit ourselves and go about fulfilling our own human potential. We now have a chance to live on our own outer limits. And we can restart *at any age* to explore our inner world.

Our creative needs are what the psychologist Maslow called self-actualization. That is when we are driven by our own internal creativeness. When we are motivated by our creative need most of the time we are living at our own outer limits. They are the basis for the excitement of exploration of the unknown, beauty and self-fulfillment.

Creativity and self-actualization are their own rewards. We must learn to expand ourselves to our outer limits. We must learn to look upon ourselves as gold mines and to mine ourselves fully. The purpose of life is to grow to the outer limits of your human potential thus maximizing the amount of creativity in your life.

If you want to become more creative start associating with those who will encourage you to try new things, to think of yourself as creative and who will applaud your endeavors. Also, read books on creativity to develop ideas that you can put to use in your life.

Continuing
Education

Many people 60 and older are familiar with Elderhostel, a national, nonprofit organization dedicated to fostering college-level educational opportunities for older learners. Elderhostel's success is phenomenal. To overcome the necessity of traveling in order to experience the excitement of challenging intellectual activity with one's peers of retirement age, the Institute Network was established. It is pledged to the advancement of another important national movement, the development of Institutes of Learning in Retirement (ILR).

An ILR is a kind of educational cooperative. People of retirement age come together to form a mini college, creating educational and social programs that are designed and managed by the members of the Institute. ILRs are almost always sponsored by a college or University.

Typical courses (often called study groups) are in the arts, sciences, and humanities. In many institutes, there are no courses taught by the faculty. The Institute relies exclusively on the talents of the members. "Peer leaders" often are not expert in the field of study, but rather serve as the coordinators for a group of co-learners, all of whom take responsibility for the reading, writing and research that goes into creating college-level learning.

In the management of an ILR the members take on essential roles in curriculum development and administration.

Institute study groups are held over a six to fifteen-week period, usually meeting once a week for about two hours. Membership dues are most often paid on a semester or annual basis, and offer the member access to several study groups and a variety of social activities.

ILRs are much more than educational programs. Social activities are an important component that bring members together in creating a dynamic, vital sense of community. Inter-generational programs and community outreach activities are the other opportunities that many Institutes incorporate. More that 70 Institutes have affiliated with the Institute Network.

Individual older learners and campus staff

are welcome to use the resources of the Institute Network to create a new ILR or enlarge the vision of an existing ILR. For full information contact: Elderhostel Institute Network, Attn: Jim Verscheren, 15 Garrison Avenue, Durham, NH 03824, (603)862-3642.

Mature Market

The Mature Market includes the 66,000,000 people who are aged 50 or over. The market is so significant that companies are hiring gerontologists to sensitize employees to the needs of an older clientele and tailor products and services for their unique requirements.

There is an emerging recognition that this market segment of people has an active life style, is healthy, is independent with a lot of free time since the children are no longer at home, well educated and well established in their communities. Similarly, a recognition is also emerging that what this population wants are social/travel opportunities, companionship, communication, coping with inflation, financial planning, transportation, health care, and a sense of being in control of their life direction.

As an example, the population of the mature market is 13 percent more likely than the average to read newspapers and to read them consistently and more thoroughly. In some geographic areas, such as that served by Florida Power and Light, nearly 30 percent of the utilities six million customers are 60 or over.

We are facing changing demographics, the likes of which have not been known before. We must use our purchasing power to change our culture for the better. Let the word go out that we will not buy products manufactured by companies that use commercials that are demeaning or reinforce the aging myth. Let's eliminate negative ads and vow to fight aging every step of the way. Let us encourage those who create a positive view of aging and help older people to lead lives of independence and dignity.

Let's eliminate negative ads for incontinence products that don't inform about and encourage, alternative therapies that eliminate the need for the products. Let's encourage the emergence of mature actors and TV commentators and particularly females 60, 65, 70 playing major roles in prime time hits.

Since market research studies indicate that we report feeling 15 years younger than our chronological age, a number that will continue to go up as the Third Age adopts vitality as a goal, advertising should be targeted to these feelings. Let's have ads that show older people as an integral part of society, part of the mainstream, with lots to offer.

Product and service companies have to recognize that the mature market is the segment of the population that is growing faster than any other and wields the strongest economic power. Americans 50 plus represent $800 billion in disposable income, $50 billion in annual travel expenditures, 50 percent of discretionary income, 40 percent of consumer demand, and 75 percent of deposits in financial institutions.

Certain banks who understand that this population uses 3.7 financial institutions concurrently with three accounts per institution, with average account balances of $6,000 and total average deposits of $66,000 have wisely, and with foresight, developed special programs to attract these depositors. The programs cater to the needs of the mature markets with such special services as free membership in AARP, social events and travel opportunities, discount offerings, insurance, car rental discounts, newsletters, and are built around the members of the mature market involvement with each other.

Some banks have involved mature customers in both the development and the operation of their programs. They are starting to recognize that free and discounted bank services are less important to mature customers than the social opportunities and a holistic concern for their welfare. Some of the most successful programs bring people together to learn, to be entertained, or to enjoy the company of others while exchanging ideas and experiences.

This market segment is so significant to banks that the Bank Marketing Association has developed a newsletter called Renaissance which tells bankers how to identify the over 50 affluent market. How to design appealing products and services, what they should and should not say in their advertising and promotions, and who is succeeding in selling to seniors both inside and outside the financial services industry.

We need products that can help us adjust to changes accompanying aging that can enhance the quality of life and preserve our independence. In some cases only a slight change in a product would make it more satisfying to older people, ie., larger instrument panels, bigger knobs.

The book that illuminates the mature market best is *Age Wave* by Ken Dychtwald and Joe Flower (catalog).

Third Age
Population

We must all have a sensitive appreciation of the rate of growth of the Third Age population so we can recognize that we are in a place that has never before existed in the history of the world.

The average life expectancy in biblical times, 2500 years ago, was 20 years. It was 1900 before it reached 43, a little more than double the span. In the last 90 years in America life expectancy has been lengthened by 33 years, one and a half times the extension that occurred during the previous 24 centuries and it equals the gain humankind made in the previous 5,000 years.

Robert N. Butler, the founding director of the National Institutes of Aging and Pulitzer Prize winning author of *Why Survive* and who now chairs the Ritter Department of Geriatrics and Adult Development at Mount Sinai School of Medicine, New York, says, "The advance in aging came about primarily as a result of success in economic progress and public health. Not only did we achieve striking reductions in maternal, childhood and infant mortality rates, but perhaps 20 percent of the gain in average life expectancy has been due to improvements associated with chronic disease and marked reduction in deaths from heart disease and stroke." For example:

94 million people are 40 or older.

66 million are 50 or older.

30 million are 65 or older.

By the year 2000, 35 million Americans will be 65 or older and approximately 108,000 will live to the age of 100. The number of Americans age 65 or older will double to 65 million by the year 2030.

Baby boomers are the 80 million Americans born between 1946 to 1965. By 2030 the oldest boomers will be 84 and the youngest 65.

The Third Age population is growing faster than any other age group and by the end of the decade it will make up a quarter of our population. The highest ratio in world history.

Baby boomers will set the agenda for the nation's public policy choices in education, work-family policies, retirement programs and health care.

Living to age 100 will be common in the next century.

We are now spending $11,000 on every American older than 65.

Last year the government spent almost 38 percent of its budget, including Social Security, on services for the elderly.

By the turn or the century, spending on the elderly will absorb approximately half of the Federal budget. This will create a fiscal crisis and result in the federal government trying to renege on all of its past promises. This aging explosion has been called the Age-Age, the Age-Wave, and the Age-Quake.

United Nations

Aging is a world wide phenomena. United Nations statisticians report that every month one million people turn 60. By 2010 the world population will have one billion older people. The United Nations recently acknowledged this global Agequake by approving the 18 principles to help countries deal with older citizens.

The United Nations Principles for Older Persons addresses issues surrounding the independence, care participation, self-fulfillment and dignity of aging people. It is the first time there has been a global recognition that the world is aging.

The United Nations principles include:

Personal autonomy in health care decision making, including the right to die with dignity by rejecting or accepting life-prolonging treatments, while diminishing life quality.

Other principles deal with the ability of older people to remain active and involved in society and to have access to legal and social services, as well as the right to be treated fairly regardless of age, race or disability.

Political
Power

I t is the voters over 50 who are the agents of
political change in America, says pollster
Andrew Kohyut, president of Princeton Survey
Research.

Ninety percent of the older population are
registered voters and two-thirds of them vote
regularly...more than any other age group. They
know more and care more about national politics
than younger people do.

While they do not generally vote in a block
they do so when it comes to Social Security and
Medicare and other age related issues.

They have the potential power at the ballot box because they represent a voting strength of 14,000,000 with the time, energy and dollars to become a significant political force. They have women of wealth who can make an impact if they decide to focus on an issue.

Seniors who make up 12.5 percent of the United States population are more than 33 percent of the voters.

Ingredients
For
Happiness

C ompanionship of peers.
A social support system from family and friends.
Some sense of individual achievement.
Some material well being.
A good self image.
Creative experiences.
A growth model as an approach to living.
A model of life based on the idea that we are capable of facing any problem and solving it through growth.
Growth is its own reward. Keep on growing

till the day you die.

Nuclear families, geographic mobility, rapid job change, high turnover rates, and the weakening of traditional values have left us adrift without the strong linkage to support groups that help build and maintain our self image.

We must aggressively act to restore support groups.

Become a joiner.

Become active within the group.

Be a friend.

You need four things: dignity, money, proper medical services and useful work. These are exactly the things you have always needed.

Financial
Planning

Planning most likely will make a big difference in the quality of life in your retirement years. Even if you have already retired, a retirement plan may be able to help you minimize taxes and help you maintain a steady income. The following section on Financial Planning was prepared by Gary Olson, a 10 year Veteran Financial Planner with IDS Financial Services, an American Express Company, Portland, Oregon.

Most of us believe that retirement is a long way down the road. You should be aware of the fact that less than half of the people who retire do so when they expect to. Many people find themselves retiring early for health, family or professional reasons and are not financially prepared.

A question often asked is "Won't the money I have in my retirement programs be enough?" Maybe not. For example, a report from the Bureau of National Affairs shows that for employees who retired on January 1, 1984 with 15 years of service and final earnings of $30,000, the average private pension benefit in 1984 was only $4,260 per year. This amount doesn't include any supplemental pension plan benefits. Also, private pension plans sometimes don't provide for automatic inflation protection after employees retire—so they may find the value of their pensions shrinking yearly.

An additional concern regarding pension plans is that often they only provide minimum benefits for the surviving spouse if an employee dies. This can be extremely important to women who generally live seven years longer than men and are often left with inadequate incomes.

A retirement plan will review your current financial situation, including Social Security and pension benefits and project how much you can expect from these sources. A financial planner can then help you determine the amount you'll need to supplement your benefits in order to live comfortably.

Another question often asked is "What should I do with my retirement money when I retire?" Depending on your retirement benefits, you probably have several options. You could take a lump sum distribution, choose monthly payments or roll your money over into a qualified account. You should consider this decision carefully and take into consideration how much income you will need to meet your monthly expenses. Your financial planner can help you determine which option is best for your personal situation.

What type of investments should you consider when planning for retirement? Perhaps the most important element in choosing appropriate investments is time. For example, if you have only five years until you retire, it may not be to your benefit to invest in a real estate partnership that will lock up your capital for 10 years.

After you retire, your main focus will most likely be on income. If you're in a high tax bracket, you'll want to look at tax management techniques. If tax relief is not an issue, you can consider a broader field of investments. Whether you're still working or are already retired, any investment you choose should fit into your overall financial plan.

Will you have to sacrifice present comforts for future security? Not necessarily. You may have to make minor adjustments in your current lifestyle to assure a comfortable retirement. However, a retirement plan may enable you to live even better during your retirement years.

Your planner also can help you determine how your retirement needs such as housing, will affect your finances. He or she can help you consider important questions you should be thinking about for estate planning and can evaluate your insurance and medical coverage to see if changes are necessary to meet your retirement needs. You've spent most of your life working toward retirement. You deserve to live comfortably and enjoy what you've been waiting for.

If you're approaching retirement or are already experiencing the benefits of retirement life, you know that every penny counts. The last thing you want to do is use your money for paying taxes on your Social Security benefits. You may not even realize that if your adjusted gross income is above a set level your Social Security benefits are, in fact, being taxed.

A portion of your Social Security benefit is included in taxable income if your adjusted gross income, plus tax-exempt income and half of your Social Security benefits, is more than the base amount. Here are the base amounts that determine whether or not your benefits are taxed. If you are married and file a joint return the base amount is $32,000. If you are married but file separate returns and did not live together during the year the base amount is $25,000. If you are single, your base amount is $25,000. The base amount for married taxpayers filing separately who lived together at any time during the year is zero.

The amount of benefits to be included in taxable income will be the lesser of one-half the benefits for the year, or one-half of the excess of your combined income—adjusted gross income plus one-half of benefits—over the base amount. Be sure you keep a record of the benefits you receive throughout the year to make figuring your taxes easier.

Depending on your financial situation, there may be certain investment products that will help you reduce your adjusted gross income and avoid being taxed on your Social Security benefits.

Annuities can be a great way to invest your money and allow it to grow tax-deferred. When an investment grows tax-deferred the earnings you receive on your investment are not taxed until they are in your possession.

For example, if you purchase an annuity, the value of the annuity will most likely increase over time. However, you will not be taxed on that increase in value until you annuitize your contract—start receiving withdrawal payments. An additional advantage is that you will most likely be in a lower tax bracket when you start your withdrawal payments.

There are several different types of annuities, but they all follow the same investment concept. An annuity is a form of a contract between the investor and the originator of the annuity, usually a life insurance company. The contract may guarantee a fixed or variable payment to the owner of the annuity some time in the future—when the owner decides to annuitize the contract and start withdrawing the investment.

If it is a fixed annuity you receive a specific dollar amount each payout period. If the value of the underlying investment declines, you will still receive the same amount each payout but the payouts may last for a shorter period of time. With a variable annuity the number of annuity units you receive each payout period is pre-determined. You will always be redeeming the same number of units but the dollar amount will vary depending on the value of the underlying investments.

If you decide to purchase an annuity, remember to consider the financial soundness of the insurance company, look at the company's rating, and the level of fees and commissions charged by the agent.

Because tax-exempt interest must be added to your adjusted gross income, all your earned interest will sooner or later be effectively taxed. If you are close to exceeding the base amount and may be forced to pay taxes on your Social Security benefits, you may want to consider moving from tax-exempt investments such as mutual fund and bonds to tax-deferred investments such as annuities, IRAs, or if you are employed, employee sponsored retirement plans.

Investments and tax issues can be very confusing. If you have questions or concerns about your financial future and the tax consequences of your investments, contact your local tax advisor or financial planner.

Self Esteem

To think well of ourselves is the central struggle of life. One of the most difficult things we have to do for ourselves is to achieve and maintain a strong self image. It is under attack throughout our life cycle in every arena.

Most people come into adulthood with self image deficiencies. Fortunately we are capable of repairing and restarting growth of our self image. However, once achieved it must continually be defended as we experience the normal buffeting of life. A poor self image impacts negatively on our psychological and physiological health. It is evidenced by excessive response to trivia and diffused hostility. We are just starting to learn the negative impact it has on the immune system.

The lack of self esteem limits us from achieving our full human potential. It motivates a negative view of life.

Make it a point every day to say something nice to yourself. Congratulate yourself on being who you are and who you can be.

Don't
Abuse It

T his book has presented the reader with a
positive view of aging and scientific
evidence that each one of us can live a long
and vital life at the outer limits of performance if
we so choose. And yet most of us, even though we
possess this new information, will not make the
commitment and devote the time and energy to
achieve the benefits described.

Our affluent culture has programmed us to
enjoy an easy and self-indulgent life. However, to
receive the benefits of an additional 20 to 30 years
of healthy and vital living you have to be prepared

to pay the price that is necessary to achieve it. You have to add an hour of hard physical activity three to five days a week, forever, to your lifestyle. You have to accept that the easy life is killing you.

Strangely, information, no mater how dramatic about the potential benefits achievable from a new lifestyle, historically has not motivated large numbers of people to change. This is because we have all suffered childhood traumas which predispose us to self destructive behavior. Women who have suffered childhood sexual molestation generally have uncontrollable needs. Innocence destroyed is never regained and as a result it is the human weakness to be self abusive, in the sense of violating our biological heritage. Even the most informed of us are guilty.

As an example, a percentage of the faculty at Harvard Medical School (a population highly informed about risk factors) continue to abuse themselves. One-half of one percent do not use seat belts; three percent continue to smoke; ten percent eat meat more frequently than the recommended guidelines; five percent eat eggs more than three times a week; seventy-two percent eat fattening deserts at least once a week, with five percent eating them over seven times a week. Thirty-nine percent fret that they have to lose weight.

These are professionals who have more information about the consequences of self defeating behavior than the general population, proving the difficulty of habit modification. You must fight the good fight every day just as everyone else must. Even if you do it imperfectly, you must fight it and try to support others in the battle.

You must recognize that with the rate of medical innovation taking place heart disease is well on the way to being understood and conquered. Cancer researchers are full of hope. There is reason to hope that even Alzheimer's disease may yield to new developments and discoveries by the year 2000. You want your body to be in shape so that you can be in condition to take advantage of these developments.

You must find the wherewithal within yourself, using your personal power or professional help if necessary to modify self defeating behavior.

Again, it is harder on women than men since as many as one third suffer childhood sexual abuse most often in incestuous settings, which predispose them to self defeating behavior for the rest of their lives. It can be mitigated with professional help. However, the consequences of the trauma, even reduced, is life long. You must use every tool available to motivate you and to create the determination to help you modify your behavior and to pay attention to risk factors and early detection.

We all, in moments of stress, momentarily backslide. This should not unfocus us from a long range view of the role of exercise and diet as being major contributors to a long a vital life. The toughest thing for anyone to do, in the absence of a clear and present danger, is to modify behavior patterns. One tool which has been found to be useful in overcoming self abuse is making an agreement with yourself just as though you were making a legal contract.

The Heart Institute at St. Vincent's Hospital and Medical Center, 9205 S. W. Barnes Road, Portland Oregon 97225, 503-291-2088, has brought the latest finding in behavioral science to bear on helping people to modify their behavior towards heart disease. Their landmark publication is entitled *It's Time For A Change Of Heart.*

It's a step by step process in which one makes a contract where you define goals in terms you can achieve and measure in relatively short time periods. Records are kept. Rewards and consequences for failure are defined. If you must, change your environment. Learn new habits. Work with others who have the same frame of mind.

Following is a summary of the Heart Institute recommendations:

1. Write Down Your Goals.

Defining a specific goal is the best way to begin to change your behavior. Make a contract with yourself to reach your goal. Put it in writing and sign it.

Begin by defining your goal in terms you can measure. Break large goals into a series of smaller goals. Spell out your responsibilities and the consequences if the action is or is not carried out (rewards and penalties). Include *start* and *review* dates. On the review dates, the contract should be rewritten and revised as necessary.

2. Keep Records.

Record keeping can make you more aware of your own behavior. Once you are aware of a problem, you can do something to change it. Record things that happen before and after the behavior you want to change.

3. Set Graduated Goals.

It is a way to make progress toward your final goal by mastering simpler behaviors first. This way, you learn desirable behavior one step at a time. Don't move to the next level until you have mastered the current one.

4. Change Your Environment.

Sometimes a change in your environment is what you need to achieve your goals. Remove temptation. Restrict the area in which undesirable behavior can happen. Make sure you have everything you need to encourage positive behavior. Remove the entertainment value from undesirable behavior. Put up visual reminders where you are most likely to need them.

5. Learn New Habits.

The goal is to fill the vacuum created by the elimination of an undesirable behavior. Replace a negative behavior with a positive one. Try distracting yourself by thinking about something pleasant. Find a healthy behavior that is opposite, or incompatible with the unhealthy one.

6. Work With Others.

Take advantage of people who are a good influence on you to make positive changes in your lifestyle. Working with others can help you keep going. Make your goals public. Let others know you want their support. Work out with groups.

7. Think Positive.

The changes we make in our own minds can be as effective as changes we make in the world around us. Tell yourself to do positive things. You can practice new behaviors in your mind. It takes time and effort to see results. Don't get discouraged.

Successful
Aging

Successful aging is accomplished by minimizing the physical negative and optimizing your personal potential. You can make dramatic changes in how well you live and you can greatly change the quality of your senior years.

Most people who are getting older fear the loss of the ability to get around easily, loss of intellect and memory and development of some lingering and painful disease. People tend to think of old age as dependence on others, inability to take care of themselves, and increasing loneliness and isolation.

Scientists have been studying slow-agers, identifying the good factors and have made observations that are instructive and inspiring to older persons. The good news is that many of these aging factors have been identified, and they can be modified.

Mobility can improve with age and this can happen regardless of the age at which exercise activity is started. The reason you can improve with age when your maximal potential is decreasing slowly each year is that you never previously functioned at you maximum ability. Few of us have ever worked at our outer limit in any area. We have physical resources we've never tapped.

You need practice to improve. Most of the crucial aspects of aging, including the presence or absence of disease, are under individual control.

We cannot change:
• Graying of hair.
• Loss of skin elasticity.
• Development of cataracts.
• Fibrosis and stiffening of arteries.
• Farsightedness.
• High-tone hearing loss.
• Elongation of ears and nose.
• Loss of subcutaneous fat in the face.
• Wrinkles of the skin.
• Failing eyesight.
We can change:
• Physical fitness.
• Heart reserve.
• Mobility.

- Blood pressure.
- Intelligence.
- Memory.
- Reaction time.
- Isolation.
- Heart disease.
- Cancer.
- Arthritis.
- Agility.

You must work to prevent the diseases that make you age faster. You must exercise your mind and your body so that the ravages of disuse do not become confused with the aging process.

As you grow older, you are more and more and more unique. There is no one else with your particular set of life experiences, insights, and beliefs. Lifetimes of widely divergent experiences create uniqueness, not conformity. The central value of age is wisdom. Wisdom results from a huge backdrop of accumulated memories and experiences that bring fresh perspective to new problems. Wisdom consists of applying experience to new situations similar in some ways to old ones frequently faced but with novel elements added.

A new characterization of age must be made. Instead of rigidity, aging provides the individual with flexibility if he keeps an open mind. Aging also means greater freedom from constraints of tight schedules and heavy personal obligations. More choice is possible, and there are more options to exercise. Aging in many ways represents freedom.

Dr. Albert Bandura, Professor of Psychology at Stanford University, has developed the concept of "self-efficacy." Self-efficacy means that you believe that you can exercise some control over events in your life. The term refers to peoples' belief in their capabilities. Effective functioning requires not only skills but the self-belief to use them well. People who believe that they can produce changes have better physical and psychological health than people who believe that nothing they can do matters.

This thinking has been applied to the development of a self-management course for patients with arthritis. In this course, patients are taught (and teach themselves) hundreds of ways to help control the problems of their arthritis through exercise, relaxation, pain management techniques, and a variety of other approaches. Individuals going through this course (now offered nationally by the Arthritis Foundation) have done much better than people who don't take the course. For many people the course plays a larger role in helping them with their arthritis than does their medication.

The major factor which correlated most strongly with decreased pain and increased function among the participants in the course was the increase in self-efficacy that resulted from the course. Patients began to recognize that their own actions could make a difference and that they could improve. *And they did.*

Course participants also learned that to be effective in self management they had to be selective in what they chose to work on. The lesson that emerged is that self management is more effective if a person optimizes his abilities in an area of particular importance to him to facilitate lifelong growth. This holds true for all of us.

People now run marathons at all ages. Marathon runners do go more slowly as they get older, about two minutes for each year over age 40. But since we have so much unused capacity the performance of the 75-year-old record marathoner is better than most 25-year-olds. Less than five percent of 25-year-olds could break the record of a 75-year-old record holder.

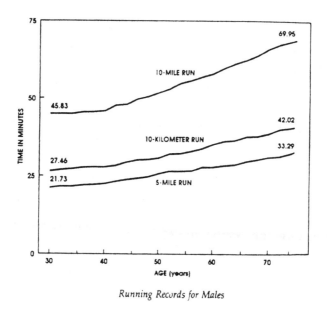

Running Records for Males

Figure 6
Printed with permission from Aging Well, copyright 1989, Addison-Wesley

The remarkable lesson is not that we run more slowly with age, but that the decline with age is so small. The ability to change at any age is a result of our plasticity. Plasticity means modifiability.

The Third Age population has many fears. They include fear of:

• Loss of the ability to get around.

• Loss of intellect and memory.

• Development of some lingering painful disease.

• Dependence on others.

• Inability to care for themselves.

• Increasing loneliness and isolation.

Two-thirds of all people want to live to be 100 but fear spending "declining" years in a nursing home or being dependent on others. Only six percent think they will make it to the century mark.

The good news is that many of the fears of the elderly can be eliminated by their own behavior.

Modifiable are:

• Isolation.

• Infirmity.

• Sickness.

• Depression.

• Increasing pain.

And two-thirds of the deaths that occur among the Third Age are postponable.

When researchers conduct large-scale psychological studies on older people, they find a special group. These are people who don't seem to have aged. They are relatively free of physical and mental problems, have solid relationships, high activity levels, are outgoing and seem well-adjusted and happy. They tend to live longer than others. About one person in seven over the age of 65 falls into this group.

They often have these things in common:

• They tend to be well-educated or come from high-level, high responsibility jobs.

• They tend to be extroverted and remain socially active.

• Their attitudes toward leisure activities, security, health and friendships are the same as those of younger people.

• They have strong feelings of being useful.

But the important factors in the makeup of these individuals appear to be habits that were cultivated and maintained throughout life. They start out mentally active, often attaining a high level of formal education, often taking on high-powered jobs. After retirement, they stay intellectually active and involved. There is a lesson for all of the Third Age in these standout people. It is that mental activity, combined with wholesome exercise, and a strong sense of contributing to the world, that makes up a formula for longevity.

Sex

If you've wondered whether a time will come in your life as you get older when sex dries up, the facts will set your mind at ease. The "basics" do not change as we grow older. Sex not only improves over time, it also is better for us. Intercourse can give us a cardiovascular workout comparable to light jogging, and it can increase our cortisol level enough to ease the pain of arthritis and help allergies. Sexual intercourse also stimulates neurotransmitters that act as natural antidepressants, analgesics and stimulants, helps prevent migraines, makes us less vulnerable to stress, renews intimacy and expresses love and affection.

Following are nuggets of information about sexual activity by age groups. As you will discover, ability to perform depends more on your state of mind than your physical capacity at any age. The death of intimacy is more destructive to a relationship than the slowing of sexuality.

The 40's

"Sexuality becomes more feminine in our 40's," say June Reihisch, Ph.D., director of the Kinsey Institute for Research in Sex, Gender and Reproduction at Indiana University.

"There's more emphasis on foreplay and less on intercourse," she says. Both men and women now need touching and time to become physically aroused. Now it's time for direct, hands-on stimulation and women want to feel "sexually necessary" as well as sexy. Men become less genitally focused and more diffusely aroused all over their bodies. Now is the time for couples to practice indulging each other in stroking and stimulation from head to toe.

When intercourse does begin, erections last minutes instead of seconds. So many women find that they become more aroused and stay aroused longer. Men who ejaculated prematurely in the 20s and 30s can now thrust longer.

The 50's

Many women now find their sexuality shifting into high gear. As estrogen levels drop, they may feel more of the sex drive created by their androgen. At 50 a woman's sex drive is often stronger than a man's. Menopause is seen as an inconvenience, not a tragedy.

Men's erections are less spontaneous, their ejaculations less explosive. The good news is that foreplay gets more attention, and more women get to have multiple orgasms.

The 60's

Erectile fullness may decrease, vaginal lubrication may decrease, frequency may decrease, but sexual satisfaction does not decrease. The trick to staying sexual past 60 has more to do with the mind than the body. Couples who want to continue making love have to see changes not as losses but as challenges.

A man does not need an erection to have an orgasm and a woman doesn't need his erection to have an orgasm either.

The 70's

A Duke University study suggests 80 percent of 70-year-olds are still interested in making love. Seventy percent of couples are having sex about once a week, as are the majority of single men. Since there are four time more widows than widowers in this age group, and two-thirds of the remaining men are married, only 25 percent of women in their seventies who feel sexual have an opportunity to make love.

Older couples luxuriate in extended mutual foreplay because erections require extended stimulation. They enjoy intercourse as much for its pleasurable sensations as for orgasm, because the male orgasm is now less explosive. They enjoy more tenderness and gentleness. Older people who prolong passion also promote health. The gerontologist, Dr. Alex Comfort, tells us, "Most people can and should expect to have sex long after they no longer wish to ride bicycles."

The 80's

According to a survey of 800 elderly couples, 75 percent of those who are still sexually active say that their lovemaking has improved. Woman who are 80 still have the capacity for orgasm. These facts come from an article by Georgia Wikin, Ph.D., an assistant clinical professor of psychiatry at Mount Sinai School of Medicine in New York City. Her sixth book *Passions* was published June, 1992.

Here are some additional miscellaneous facts that report on numbers of men and women alive in certain age groups and new sexual and companion relationships being investigated:

One million nine hundred thousand older couples live together without being married.

For every 100 women between the ages of 65-69 there are 83 men.

After 85 there are only 42 men alive for every 100 women.

In 1984 there were 10.4 million single women over 65 but only 2.7 million single men over 65.

Three million American women are married

to men who are at least 10 years younger than they are.

Share-a-man arrangements are found on some cruise lines which use older male "hosts." In exchange for their nonsexual services, the host receives free cruise passage, complimentary shore excursions, and $100 bar credit per trip. Hosts dine with ladies, dance with them, join them on shore excursions, and make sure everyone is having a good time.

The Starr-Weiner Report on older sexuality showed that 38.7 percent of older Americans would like to try new sexual experiences, and 9.9 felt that women should deal with the shortage of men through "maverick arrangements" such as several women sharing a man.

In *Ourselves, Growing Older* by Paula Brown Doress and Diana Lasking Siegal and the Midlife and Older Woman Book Project (catalog), a book dedicated to women aging with knowledge and power, they report the following:

At least 10 percent or more of women are lesbian. There is a need by them for nonsexual touching to express tenderness and affection, to acknowledge each other's presence nonverbally, to comfort, to support and to soothe.

The authors report a recent study of people 60 to 91 years old which revealed that 91 percent enjoyed sex for a variety of reasons. Among the reasons listed were: Sex reduces tension, makes women feel more feminine, helps people sleep, provides a physical outlet for emotions. The people studied engaged in sexual relations an average of

1.4 times a week, about what they averaged when they were in their forties.

Both Kinsey and Masters and Johnson found that women and men continue their accustomed sexual patterns throughout their later years. The researchers confirmed what many women have discovered for themselves, that there is no time limit on women's sexual capacities. Although women's responses may slow down they can continue to enjoy sex and orgasm throughout their lives. Women can be sexual in a variety of ways, with a man or a woman, or by pleasuring themselves.

Older people report in several studies that oral sex is a favorable activity. Cuddling, caressing, and manual stimulation are also satisfying. Lovemaking may continue to be satisfying whether one, both, or neither party has an orgasm. Many older women are enjoying sex aides. Women find vibrators more effective stimulation than men do, and prefer electric vibrators that are not shaped like a phallus. These prove intense stimulation to the nerve endings around the vulva and clitoris.

James F. Fries, M.D. in his book *Aging Well* (catalog) reports: "The essence of human sexuality is warmth and contact with others. Don't be afraid to hug your friends, your children, or your grandchildren socially. The physical parts of sex are electives, not requirements. Freedom from the sexual pressures allows a greater range of choice."

In 1984 Edward Brecher edited a famous report for the Consumer's Union entitled *Love, Sex and Aging*. The study reported on 4,246 individuals ranging from 50 to 93. The report disclosed that the following percentage of women were sexually active:

93 percent of women in their 50's

81 percent of women in their 60's

65 percent of women in their 70's

The corresponding figures for sexually active men were as follows:

98 percent of men in their 50's

91 percent of men in their 60's

79 percent of men in their 70's

Twenty four out of the 46 men over the age of 80 reported that they were still having intercourse while 15 out of the 38 women over 80 reported still having intercourse.

In 1986, Judy Bretschneider and Dr.Norma Coy of the Department of Psychology at San Francisco State University, published a paper entitled *Sexual Interest and Behavior in Healthy 80-102 Year Olds*. It reported that 88 percent of the men and 71 percent of the women of the 202 subjects studied indicated that they still had intimate thoughts about the opposite sex. Seventy two percent of the men and 40 percent of the women masturbated, and 63 percent of the men and 30 percent of the women still had sexual intercourse.

In a recent survey of members of a Fifty Plus Running club in Palo Alto, California, who are over 70, 25 of the 32 respondents reported that sexual activity was still fair or good. As our culture becomes more liberal towards sex in the Third Age it is reasonable to expect that all of the reported statistics on sexual activity will indicate greater participation in sex at older ages.

Alex Comfort in the *A Good Age* reports that aging induces some changes in human sexual performance. These are chiefly in the male, for whom orgasm becomes less frequent. More direct physical stimulation is also needed to produce an erection. However these changes are functionally minimal and actually tend in the direction of greater, if less acute, satisfaction for both partners. Sexual requirement and sexual capacity are lifelong. Even if and when actual intercourse is impaired by infirmity, other sexual needs persist, including closeness, sensuality and being valued as a man or as a woman. This positive view of aging sexuality may be contrary to the beliefs of some older people who have been convinced that sexual capacity dries up after age 60. Actually, as far back as 1926 the biostatistician Raymond Pearl found that four percent of all males between the ages of seventy and seventy-nine were having intercourse every third day, and another nine percent were having it as least weekly. For those who have been happily active in youth, age abolishes neither the need nor the capacity nor the satisfaction, unless illness compromises their ability to enjoy sex, or deprives them of a partner.

Almost certainly the new old will be more active into later years because they have grown up living sexually, view sex positively, and have not aged in the folklore expectations of impotence and continence but in the determination to go on as long as possible in the style they have known.

The first step in preserving your sexuality, which for many people is an aspect of preserving their personhood, is to realize that, if cultivated, sexuality can be, and normally is, lifelong in both sexes. Sex is a non-dangerous activity. Stopping it unwillingly, due to being frightened after an illness, is far more dangerous to health than a little exertion; in some people stopping leads to severe depressions.

It's proper to use any means to stay active and to avoid sloppiness at any age, but don't be exploited by people who minister to your insecurities or sell you on your fears. Sex follows upon how you are, not how you look. An experienced man would wish to have sex with a woman of any age close to his own who experiences herself as a fully sexual person.

It has been shown that the residential care homes which follow the sexual mores of the outside world, have happier and less deteriorated residents, and a vastly lower consumption of tranquilizers, than the conventional "home." It was Harry Golden, the southern newspaper columnist and author, who observed to his wife when she apologized the morning after, "It's all right. Even when it's not good, it's not so bad."

This is not the end of a section of the book. We hope it is the beginning for you of new insights and new relationships and the reexamination of old ones. We wish you all the joys life has to offer, all the joys you wish for yourself.

Embrace yourself - embrace your lover - embrace your powers.

Centenarians

Centenarians are interesting to observe in order to further our understanding of "aging." As a group they seem to have outlived old age, because far fewer show the disease processes and chronic disabilities that kill most people before they reach the century mark.

Mortality flattens for this group. They are pictures of what "aging" without disease, would be like. Belle Boone Beard, a Georgia sociologist, wrote a book in 1967 about several hundred reputed American centenarians. Questioned about their health, 17 percent said excellent, 39 percent good,

33 percent fair, six percent poor and only three percent very poor. These centenarians were fully engaged in life-driving, working where they were permitted to work and scoring higher than average on the social space they occupied.

The general impression is that centenarians have a psychic component which gives them the advantage to age without illness because they are psychologically hardy and can shake off adversity.

Natural Death

With the elimination of infectious diseases and the avoidance or postponement of chronic disease by healthy life styles, dying of natural causes will become the norm. Our organs have seven to eleven times the capacity required for normal functioning when we are born. This provides protection and survival when we are exposed to stress.

As an example, during exercise the heart can increase its output more than six times. But, as we age we lose part of our reserve capacity. At age 85 less than 50 percent remains. We need at least 30 percent to continue to function. Random stress which exceeds the remaining reserve results in death. This is what is meant by natural death.

The rate of decline of organ reserve can be slowed by changes in lifestyle. Since we have never had a population that rigorously observed risk factors and used diet, exercise and early detection of disease to ward off death, it is hard to predict the total outcome. All of the current indications are very positive.

We have the opportunity to be vital for our entire life span and die a natural death. Thirty additional years, with the full possession of individual powers is potentially available to us all, provided we pay our dues.

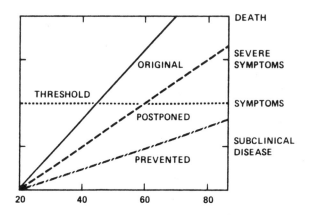

Figure 7

The clinical course of chronic disease. The universal, chronic diseases begin early in life, progress through a clinical threshold, and eventuate in disability or death. An important strategy for their control is to alter the rate at which they develop, thus postponing the clinical illness or even preventing it.

Two thirds of deaths are postponable.

If we practice all we know now, we could postpone 1,260 deaths each year. It could be yours that is postponed.

Printed with permission from *Vitality And Aging*, Copyright 1981, W. H. Freeman and Company.

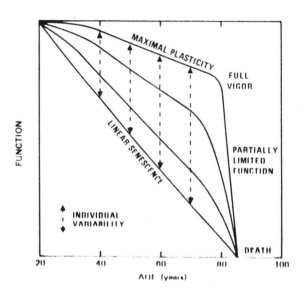

Figure 8

The individual rectangular curves for vigor, representing a lifetime of vigor followed by terminal collapse.

Printed with permission from *Vitality And Aging* 1982, W.H. Freeman and Company.

MODIFIABLE ASPECTS OF AGING

Aging Marker	Personal Decision(s) Required
Cardiac reserve	Exercise, nonsmoking
Dental decay	Prophylaxis, diet
Glucose tolerance	Weight control, exercise, diet
Intelligence test	Training, practice
Memory	Training, practice
Osteoporosis	Weight-bearing exercise, diet
Physical endurance	Exercise, weight control
Physical strength	Exercise
Pulmonary reserve	Exercise, nonsmoking
Reaction time	Training, practice
Serum cholesterol	Diet, weight control, exercise
Skin aging	Sun avoidance
Systolic blood pressure	Salt limitation, exercise, weight control

Printed with permission from *Vitality And Aging* 1982, W.H. Freeman and Company.

Use It
Or
Lose It

D r. Walter M. Bortz II, M.D., author of *We Live Too Short And Die Too Long* subtitled *How to Achieve and Enjoy Your Natural 100-Year-Plus Life Span* is the person who has collected all of the scientific evidence to establish the validity of Use It Or Lose It (catalog).

Dr. Bortz is one of America's most respected and acclaimed authorities on aging. He is the former president of the American Geriatrics Society with over 35 years of clinical experience. He co-chaired the AMA-ANA task force on aging and is presently clinical associate professor at

Stanford University Medical School. He practices what he preaches. He and his wife are both marathoners.

He has worked with thousands of patients over 85 and knows the reality of the aging process first hand. His definition of our moment in history is the "Age Age."

He has labeled all of the consequences of the lack of use as the "Disuse Syndrome" which includes cardiovascular deterioration, fragility, obesity and depression. When our bodies were first developed in the era in which we came out of the trees and onto the plains, hunters ran animals to exhaustion and then killed them. Bushman today use the same methodology. As a result their natural activity keeps them fit throughout their lifetime, with the resultant benefits of avoidance of the chronic diseases that plague our culture. And medical theory indicated that the robustness of any bone is in direct proportion to the physical stress placed on it.

Neanderthal bones, 60,000 years old, are tremendously massive, comparable to iron ingots next to our fragile bones. Analysis of the bones of present aboriginal people show that they are similarly much more rugged than our own. There are no broken hips due to osteoporosis in the jungles of Borneo. There are no obese bush-men.

Dr. Bortz's experience with native populations, including members in their late 60's was that the normal course of their daily routine keeps them physically fit and well.

Our physical heritage was first eroded by

the Agricultural Revolution and still further by the Industrial Revolution. Now the Information Revolution is taking us another step towards even more inactivity. The experience with marathon runners demonstrates that a fit person of 70 has the same oxygen carrying capacity of an unfit person of 30. It should be obvious that our standards for the measurement of what is normal is based on measuring a population that is not living up to its biological potential. As an example, what is the normal size of coronary arteries? That which we measure in an unexercised population or that which we measure in marathon runners which are two to three times larger.

Recent studies at Stanford have demonstrated that exercise expands the coronary arteries. It is well known that confinement to bed in a hospital for four to six weeks produces the same amount of calcium loss from bones as seen in ten years of so called normal aging.

Dr. Bortz also reports that the lack of gravity in space reduces the use of muscles with the resultant apparent weakness on the return to earth. The introduction of exercise equipment usage during a flight was a result. Also, inactivity leads to depression. Studies have shown that exercise is one of the effective treatments for depression. Fitness becomes more important to survival and quality of life the older we get.

Vital Women
In Their 70s,
80s, And 90s

C ecelia Hurwich, of Berkely, California,
completed a decade of research and
received her doctorate in life-span
development psychology upon submitting her
dissertation, *Vital Women In Their Seventies,
Eighties, and Nineties: A Longitudinal Study* when
she was 70 years old.

It resulted from 100 in-depth interviews
with older women. One noteworthy theme stood
out as common to them all: It was not the events of
their lives but how they perceived those events that
determined their sense of well-being. The women

she studied taught her that tremendous opportunities still exist for growth at advanced age and for developing latent potentials in the individual. She discovered that a woman's positive expectations about aging influenced her health and well-being and that, although her years were limited, she had a lot of living to do.

Here are the five keys to vital aging that Hurwich discovered in her 10 years of research:

1. Living in the present with compelling interests or work, creative activity, and friends.

2. Continued growth, which helps one experience life as meaningful.

3. Optimistic attitude and positive expectations.

4. Close relationships with people of all ages.

5. Remaining in one's own home.

There are factors mitigating against women fulfilling themselves in the five ways listed and it is worthwhile to review them before addressing methods to obtain the keys to vital aging.

Because of our culture's programming towards youth and beauty aging is much harder on women than on men. It happens to women earlier, is combined with sexism, and permeates all of their lives. Women, on the average, live seven years longer than men. After 65 there are only 2.7 million single men to provide companionship to 10.4 million women.

Half of all women over 65 are widows. Only 40 percent of older women are married and living with their husbands. After 85 there are only

42 men alive for every 100 women. Since women are orgasmic and retain sexuality till they die, it becomes necessary to examine options for alternative relationships. We all need care and company and social support that comes with a chosen life style among friends in a compatible environment and community.

What are older women's choices for companionship:

1. Marry younger men. Historically this has been frowned on by our culture and our children.

2. Share men with other women. This has produced social humiliation, although share-a-man arrangements on cruise lines have become somewhat popular. The cruise line retains male "Hosts" who dine, dance, and join women in shore excursions and make sure everyone has a good time. Extended sharing relationships are not common as yet.

3. Group living with other women also has significant economic benefits. Living in companionships can help reduce the health risks of living alone. There is a kind of nonintrusive responsibility that sort of grows by just being in close proximity to another human. With the passing of the extended family and the lengthening of life expectancy, this kind of non-familial, yet personal close support, may be a welcome substitute especially for those in the 70s, 80s and beyond.

4. Lesbian relationships are socially frowned upon.

5. Live with children and grandchildren as in the past. Emotional needs are the glue that holds

families together replacing the economic needs of the past. Increasingly, this has not proved to be satisfactory.

Among the pluses emerging for women are these findings:

In the realm of sex women age better than men. Age related hormonal changes do not result in any significant alteration in arousal time or the ability to achieve sexual orgasm.

Work is just as beneficial to women as to men in terms of increased longevity and vitality. A recent study by University of California researchers indicates that working women have a significantly lower risk of heart disease, the nation's leading killer of women, than homemakers or women who could not find steady work. The study should prove reassuring for women who want to work.

According to the study, working women, managers, business owners, professionals, executives, secretaries and administrators had sharply lower total cholesterol and blood sugar levels, two of the key indicators for heart disease as well as better numbers on other heart related risk factors. In all, the women had a healthy lifestyle drinking and smoking less, weighing less, and exercising more than women at home.

Women hear better than men.

The Older Women's League (OWL), a grass-roots, national organization, was created in 1981 to fight the impact of ageism with the view of correcting the financial, medical and social problems older women face.

In this society men die significantly earlier

than women and women have more illnesses than men. Neither condition has to exist. In an ideal environment male female mortality differences are narrowed to genetic difference and the environmental differences are minimized.

But since women are sicker they take more drugs. As we age, drug side effects and drug interactions are magnified. As a result, women suffer a host of negative effects which they have been programmed to believe are mental rather than physical or prescription drug related. And since many have been abused and have low self esteem they are prepared to accept the blame as their own fault.

In 1850 a mother's last child married when she was 59, two years before the mean age at death. By 1950 the youngest of a mother's children married when she was 48, with more than 30 years of life ahead of her.

Since most women living on retirement or widow's benefits lived in an era when stigma was attached to living unmarried in sin they feel stigmatized if they do so and cannot live freely or happily in such a circumstance. Insecurity is ever present since the relationship is not formalized by contract.

Women in this framework are pressured by the children of both partners because of inheritance concerns. And the woman cannot let go of her fears caused by her sense of impermanence.

Women have to learn that the guilt of parenting still infects all relationships. It is time for women to lay responsibility on adult children and have them understand that mother has a life of her own. Freed from guilt-ridden ambivalent parent-child conflicts, the woman can pursue a life style where only her goals, needs, desires and dreams need to be considered—a time for herself.

Women have to go beyond the need to be needed and realize they need themselves as much as anyone has needed them. Her time is now with children grown, independent and with families and values of their own. Women can have as much or little as they desire.

The self esteem of women divorced or abandoned will be submerged in or shattered by anger and resentment. To encourage them to pursue remarriage is to ask them to enter a competition that many have neither the desire nor the energy to undertake. While more than half of women over 65 are widowed, only one out of seven men of the same age is a widower, and four times as many women as men in this category live alone.

Also women past 68 have been socialized to view other women as competitors for a husband. This competition really heats up after 60 and the rivalry sharpens.

Instead of viewing other women in an adversarial role they should be looked upon as a resource for the future life style an individual woman hopes to achieve. Alternate lifestyles are discussed in this section and reflect new ways of living.

Eleanor Roosevelt, recognized as one of history's most significant women was asked late in her life what she would have asked for if she could have made a wish come true. Her reply was "To have been born beautiful." Her dissatisfaction with her appearance and accompanying insecurity overshadowed and diminished, to herself, her magnificent lifetime achievements. It is how women perceive themselves that makes the difference in their lives, as Cecelia Hurwich discovered in her interviews of 100 women. But women do have an uphill battle because of attitudes in our culture towards beauty and youth. Typical is the classic stereotype: "Men mature, Women get old." Ageism happens to women earlier, is combined with sexism and both inhabit and inhibit all phases of a woman's life. Women must begin sooner, and sustain longer, a self fulfillment dedicated to a quality of life that will be enriching and rewarding all their years. Since the average woman has been programmed to believe she needs men for "Social Security" and acceptance, she must address other options for lifestyles that reflect new social arrangements. New ideas for living are essential because women far outlive men in the advanced years. Most women realize that the most destructive thing they can do to themselves is to become lonely from lack of companionship. Loneliness leads to depression.

Some lifestyle ideas violate the encultured sense of morality in our society. But it is women who have always been more adventurous in social change. Women must be open to the unknown, unexperienced and unapproved life choices.

Caretaking Alternatives

The degree and scale of new living arrangements will, of course, depend on what financial position a woman finds herself in. What does she need for financial security, personal happiness and strong relationships with others? She may be able to find a cooperative arrangement and pay only the small price of giving up part of her privacy to alleviate loneliness.

Among the living alternatives that have been suggested is one in which a small and well selected group have contracted to pool all resources, financial, physical, and emotional for their mutual well being. The contract is detailed to suit the group need, current and future, and will include caretaking if and when necessary.

Sample Group

1. Woman with a large house and grounds.
   A. Skills: homemaking, shopping, cooking.
   B. Mobility: drives, active, high energy.
   C. Financial: a small monthly income.
   D. Needs: companionship, privacy and financial aid.
2. Woman with a small apartment.
   A. Skills: homemaking, sewing, knitting.
   B. Mobility: limited, does not drive, walks, moderate energy.
   C. Financial: respectable monthly income.
   D. Needs: companionship, transportation, nutrition.

3. Man with a small apartment.
   A. Skills: handy with tools, gardens, shops.
   B. Mobility: drives, walks, moderate energy.
   C. Financial: excellent finance.
   D. Needs: companionship, nutrition, homemaking services.

These three can adapt to group living very well since all needs and all skills are compatible. The contract would necessitate that a dollar value be established on all services to be interchanged to better equalize contributions. If this type of living style proves successful it should evolve into a relationship of he who needs gets and he who gets returns. As the relationship becomes comfortable, grows and flourishes the need for equalizing contributions will become variable.

<u>Economic Disadvantage of Women</u>

It is important for women to take economic control of their lives says Christopher L. Hayes, executive director of the National Center for Women and Retirement Research at Long Island University in Southampton, N.Y. Talking about women and investing, he says "If we are truly going to eradicate another generation of women being impoverished in their old age, we have to get to women in their 20s and 30s, when they get their first job."

The nonprofit center gets many calls from women who want information on how to invest wisely. (The centers number is: (516)283-4000 ext.

266) In too many cases, women have reached their fifties having had someone else make all the investment choices for them. All of a sudden, through death or divorce, the decision maker may be gone.

On top of enduring a traumatic loss, the woman then has to decide what to do with the payout from her husband's pension plan, the lump-sum divorce settlement or certificates of deposit maturing soon. The only way for women to guard against that scenario is to become investment savvy.

It's more critical than ever for women to take control of their long-term finances. Among the reasons:

Women outlive men, and midlife divorces have tripled in the last decade. The result is a burgeoning group of women who will have to fund their own retirement. More than half of all U.S. women older than 18, almost 54 million, now work outside the home. Yet those who work full-time still earn 74 cents for every dollar earned by men. And less than half of those working women have pensions.

Aging Well

Women who want to age well must recognize that to do so requires more than the absence of disease. It is a harmony of mind, body, and spirit. Each woman can take an active role in her well-being as she ages—a holistic approach that involves sharing with others, reducing stress, and participating in community, among other avenues.

Women can prolong their healthy active years by paying attention to good nutrition, activity and movement, solitude and rest, good relationships, and with links to the communities in which they live and work. It is especially important to distinguish physical aging, which one can do something about, from the capacity for intellectual growth and social participation which can be expanded.

A wellness program requires effort, planning and persistence, but it is an investment that pays back with unbelievably high interest.

We have the power to enrich our lives and those of others through our personal relationships. Research has shown that those who maintain strong bonds with family, friends, or neighbors actually have lower death and illness rates. When a woman feels isolated, it takes courage and initiative on her part to reach out to make friends. A ten-year study of seven thousand people across the nation found that the mortality rate among people with poor social bonds was 2.5 times higher than among people with a good support system of friends and relatives. Aloneness causes melancholia and melancholia causes death.

See *When Women Retire*, Carole Sinclair (catalog).

Overthrow
Ageism

Our culture has begun to change attitudes relative to ageism. Cultural change can be compared to a plague. First a few people are infected. They in turn infect a few more, then, all at once, an epidemic.

Now is the time for all of us to jump on the bandwagon and participate in the overthrow of ageism. The groundwork of recognition of the problem has taken place, the emergence of legislation setting up social sanctions against it has occurred and enough examples of those who resist the myth exists.

Indicative of the changes taking pace is the recent popularity of actors aged 60, 65, 70 and older who are playing prime roles in both TV and the movies.

To keep Angela Lansbury, 66, happy and healthy, her contract calls for her to work four 12-hour days a week on "Murder, She Wrote." She says, "I think it's terribly important that women my age maintain their vigor and their energy. I'm not going to retire. Most women actresses don't ever retire."

James Garner, 63, who has arthritis, and can no longer handle physically demanding parts, has just started a new TV series.

John Forsythe, 73, has returned to prime time in a new half-hour sitcom for NBC.

Beatrice Arthur 65, Betty White 69, Ossie Davis 74, Hal Holbrook 66, Charles Durning 68, William Conrad 72, Brian Keith 71, James Arness 69, Carrol O'Connor 68, Johathan Winters 67, Peter Falk 65, Edward Asner 63 are indicative of the move to more visible representation of the Third Age population in the public eye.

Department of Labor statistics indicate that the number of Third Age entrepreneurs has increased 12 percent between 1981 and 1991. The future for the older population is starting to look bright. We can expect to live longer and healthier lives. We are becoming more visible in terms of numbers and political activism.

We can have a choice between: creative activities, entrepreneurship, leisure retirement, protest retirement, and acceptance retirement.

In his book, *Why Survive?* Robert N. Butler laid down an Agenda for Activism in 1975 related to aging. It included a very detailed program whose section headings are:

- Consciousness raising.
- Political Activity including running for office.
- Community Activity.
- Registration Drives.
- Grievance Activity.
- Collective Activity.
- Resistance Activity.
- Protective Activity.
- Surveillance Activity.
- Cooperative Activity.
- Communications and Education.
- Whistle Blowing.

One example of activism is stamping out ageist remarks. Behavioral psychology teaches that if you alter people's verbal behaviors you alter them. No broad based national organization has fulfilled Butler's agenda to date. It still needs to be done. The choices facing the 66,000,000 persons over 50 are either to convert AARP into this type of organization or form a new one. It is time to form a movement to grant the aged more rights and privileges and a greater chance for a fulfilling life.

How the growing number of mature people in the Third Age will affect ageism will depend on whether they organize for social action and become visible in the society at large. We have to focus on breaking the negative stereotypes. We have to draw attention to the older people who are making significant contributions today.

Healthy, successful aging can be achieved with a minimum of physical and mental disability.

We can fulfill our human potential, live at our outer limits and exploit our lifetime potential for physical strength and for a richer emotional intellectual and social life. We can be complete human beings throughout our entire life span.

People in the Third Age run marathons, go back to college, are entrepreneurial and start up new business, are late bloomers in every field of endeavor, and not just the arts, and experience creative highs by doing new things.

They now freely participate in activities which in the past were considered to belong exclusively to the young.

We must focus on not what is but what can be.

Organizations

The Older Women's League, (membership 20,000) 730 Eleventh Street, N.W., Suite 300, Washington, D.C. 20001 (202)783-6686 is a grass-roots, national organization created in 1980 to change the plight of older women in the United States. It set out to correct medical and social problems older women face.

OWL champions such issues as ensuring equal wages, disparity in employment hiring and job-training practices. The league helps women to stay in control of their own lives to the end of life.

OWL's 120 chapters nationwide have made

substantial progress. They helped get the Group Health Insurance Continuation Act passed in 1986. It provides for unemployed, disabled, widowed or divorced people to continue paying the same rate of group insurance for up to three years after leaving an employment rather than the normal 18 months. OWL is really an organization for women who believe in making changes.

The Gray Panthers (70,000 members) were formed by Maggie Kuhn and five of her friends in 1970 when they were forcibly retired at age 65. The organization is based in Washington, D.C. and its address and phone number are: 1424 16th Street, N.W., Suite 602, Washington, D.C. 20036 (202)387-3111.

A consciousness-raising, activist group of older adults and young people, the Gray Panthers aims are to combat ageism. It espouses the belief that both the old and the young have much to contribute to make our society more just and humane.

It is a militant organization which has demonstrated at meetings of the American Medical Association and the National Gerontological Society, monitored municipal agencies, liberated men and women from unsafe nursing homes and organized a Media Watch to eliminate all ageist programs and commercials from the air.

The National Alliance of Senior Citizens, 2525 Wilson Blvd., Arlington, Virginia 22201 (703)528-7380 was organized to inform the membership and the American public of the needs of senior citizens and of the programs and policies being carried out by the government and other specified groups. It represents the views of senior Americans before Congress and state legislatures.

The National Council Of Senior Citizens (membership 4,500,000) was founded by the AFL-CIO during the fight for Medicare and was widely credited with defeating the lobbyists of the American Medical Association. It has 4,000 local chapters. It is a grass-roots organization focusing on political and legislative issues and keeps track of Congressional voting records.

The American Association of Retired Persons (membership 30,000,000) 601 E Street N.W., Washington, D.C. 20049 (202)434-2277 is an organization representing the interest of persons over 50. In 1987 AARP successes included pension-reform legislation amended into the tax bill and helped to end mandatory retirement based on age. It has a legislative staff of 125 and now has 20 lobbyists working full time to influence Congress.

The political power of AARP rises from the fact that it can speak for those 30 million members and from the fact that it has 350,000 active volunteers with a presence in every state.

Aging
On Hold

B ecause of the significance of the book *Aging On Hold* (catalog), we have given it an extensive review. Much of the material in this section is based on information in the book which has developed some startling facts about the reversing and manipulation of aging by science. Readers are encouraged to buy the book in order to fully appreciate its potential impact on their present and future lifestyles.

Long life with the retention of youthful vigor is humanity's oldest dream. Now it seems such a goal is not only possible, but probable. The modern scientific quest for longevity recently occupied *Chicago Tribune* science writers Ronald Kotulak and Peter Gorner for more than a year, culminating in their ground breaking series of articles, *Aging On Hold* which appeared in the *Tribune* December 8 to 15, 1991. The writers' investigations took them to dozens of aging research scientists in the United States and Europe who are involved in exciting discoveries about how good health and longevity can be extended.

Material from *Aging On Hold* is summarized here. It is the first book that offers a comprehensive tour of the new frontier in medical science in which researchers boldly endeavor to retard and even reverse human aging, and succeed. According to Kotulak and Gorner, aging is a complex process, and research findings suggest that no single theory can explain it. Current scientific thinking now theorizes that aging is the result of both genetic and environmental processes. The goal of aging research is to prevent, delay or reverse aging and to help people avoid infirmity as long as possible until they die after an extended, healthy, vigorous life from truly natural causes.

The tool kit the scientists have built in the laboratories to develop anti-aging benefits include nutrition, exercise, drug therapy and genetic engineering. The discoveries reported in *Aging On Hold* range from pioneering experiments on the cellular level, to simple techniques that anyone can start using to live longer.

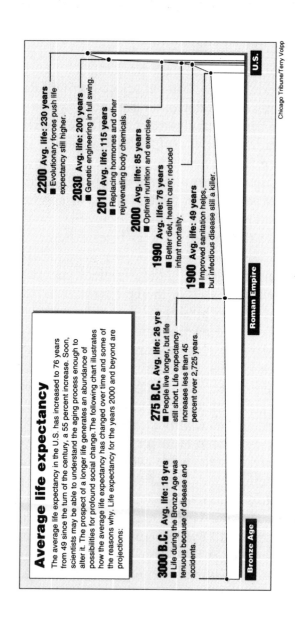

Average life expectancy

The average life expectancy in the U.S. has increased to 76 years from 49 since the turn of the century, a 55 percent increase. Soon, scientists may be able to understand the aging process enough to alter it. The prospect of a longer life generates an abundance of possibilities for profound social change. The following chart illustrates how the average life expectancy has changed over time and some of the reasons why. Life expectancy for the years 2000 and beyond are projections:

3000 B.C. Avg. life: 18 yrs
■ Life during the Bronze Age was tenuous because of disease and accidents.

275 B.C. Avg. life: 26 yrs
■ People live longer, but life still short. Life expectancy increases less than 45 percent over 2,725 years.

1900 Avg. life: 49 years
■ Improved sanitation helps, but infectious disease still a killer.

1990 Avg. life: 76 years
■ Better diet, health care; reduced infant mortality.

2000 Avg. life: 85 years
■ Optimal nutrition and exercise.

2010 Avg. life: 115 years
■ Replacing hormones and other rejuvenating body chemicals.

2030 Avg. life: 200 years
■ Genetic engineering in full swing.

2200 Avg. life: 230 years
■ Evolutionary forces push life expectancy still higher.

Bronze Age

Roman Empire

U.S.

Chicago Tribune/Terry Volpp

Figure 9
Reprinted with permission from *Aging On Hold,* Copyright
1992 Tribune Publishing

Turning Back The Biological Clock

A Veterans Administration recent one year experiment with 27 male volunteers who received weekly injections of genetically engineered human growth hormone demonstrates the potential of reversing the aging process. The volunteers regained 20 years of lost vigor. Flabby skin became taut. Soft muscles hardened. Fat melted away. Internal organs shrunken by age resumed their youthful size and vigor.

Projects that scientists worldwide are pressing in the quest for youth and longevity include:

Drugs that prolong youthfulness.

Revolutionary strategies of nutrition and exercise.

Root causes of chronic disease—cancer, osteoporosis, Alzheimer's—are being understood and new methods for early detection, prevention and cure are being developed and tested.

Sharply restricted food intake in animals is resulting in a startling increase in longevity up to twice the normal life span. This evidence holds great promise for humans who may be able to defer aging by controlling calorie intake and watching diet closely. The overwhelming conclusion of all of the evidence is that for the most part aging is reversible.

There are three ways of staving off the aging process according to the authors of *Aging On Hold:*

Lifestyle changes.

Better diets, exercise and a healthier lifestyle. Doing this could enable most people to live to be about 85.

Tune ups

It is boldly estimated that through periodic tune ups of bodies and brains by replacing the body's hormones, growth factors, and chemical defense systems people could routinely live up to 115 years.

Genetics

Life will be extended by intervention with drugs and gene therapy at the biochemical level. Some scientists predict life spans of 200 years and beyond.

Aging On Hold recommends taking a broad-based, multivitamin, multi-mineral supplement formulated at one to two times the RDA as a conservative and rational thing for older people to do.

The Hopes And Fears Of Extending Life

Putting aging on hold is no longer the wild dream of crackpot scientists playing with monkey gland extracts in clandestine laboratories. Aging research, centering on retarding the effects of growing older physically, is being pressed on several exciting fronts with advances being made almost daily. People who wish to turn back the clock will benefit directly from the research as new medicines reach the market. But there are methods to retard aging available to all of us now and they are explained at length in *Aging On Hold*.

The new visionaries of science, biogerontologists, envision a world where people stay healthier longer and the wisdom of experience accumulates in those still in their prime. The world needs experience combined with the vigor of youth to meet the profound problems of the future. The Third Age may prove to be the Golden Age for generations now and those to come.

Controlling aging

*10 ways to help retain youth and
postpone the onset of aging.*

1 Muscle mass: Americans tend to lose 6.6 pounds of lean body mass each year, with the rate accelerating after age 45. **Control factor: Exercise.**

2 Strength: The average person loses 30 percent of muscles and nerves between ages 20 and 70. Strength and size of remaining cells can be increased. **Control factor: More exercise.**

3 Calories: At age 70 a person needs 500 fewer calories per day to maintain body weight. **Control factor: Reduce calorie intake.**

4 Body fat: The average 65-year-old sedentary woman's body is 43 percent fat compared to 25 percent at age 25. **Control factor: Convert fat into muscle by exercising.**

5 Blood pressure: Most Americans show an increase in blood pressure with age. **Control factor: Exercise.**

6 Blood-sugar tolerance: Some diabetes cases are caused by an increase in body fat and loss of muscle mass. **Control factors: Exercise; diet.**

7 Cholesterol: Bad cholesterol leads to heart disease, good cholesterol helps protect against it. **Control factors: Low fat diet; exercise.**

8 Temperature: The body's ability to regulate temperature declines with age. **Control factors: Regular exercise; diet.**

9 Bone density: Bones lose mineral content and become weaker with age. **Control factors: Proper calcium; stress exercise.**

10 Aerobic capacity: The body's efficient use of oxygen declines by 30-40 percent by age 65. **Control factor: Aerobic exercise.**

Sources: 'Biomarkers' by William Evans, PH.D. and Irwin H. Rosenberg, M.D.

Figure 10
Reprinted with permission, from *Aging On Hold*,
Copyright 1992 Tribune Publishing.

Bibliography

Age Wave, Ken Dychtwald, Ph.D. and Joe Flower, 1990, Bantam Books.

Aging On Hold, Ronald Kotulak and Peter Gorner, 1992, Tribune Publishing.

A Good Age, Alex Comfort, 1976, Simon and Schuster.

A Good Old Age, Paul Homer and Martha Holstein, 1990, Simon and Schuster.

Aging Parents, 1988, PNW 246, A Pacific Northwest Extension Publication.

Aging Well, James F. Fries, M.D., 1989, Addison-Wesley.

Aging Well, Thomas Hager and Laureen Kessler, 1987, Simon and Schuster.

Americans Over 55, At Work Program Research Reports 1 & 2, Published January 25, and March 8, 1990, The Commonwealth Fund.

Avoid The Aging Trap, Muriel Oberleder, Ph.D., 1982, Acropolis.

Biomarkers, William Evans, Ph.D. and Irwin H. Rosenberg, M.D., 1991, Simon and Schuster.

Creative Aging, Mary Baird Carlsen, 1991, W.W. Norton and Company.

Creativity In Business, Michael Ray and Rochelle Myers, 1986, Doubleday.

Enjoy Old Age, B.F. Skinner and M.E. Vaughn, 1983, W.W. Norton and Company.

Enabling Older Americans To Work, Reprinted from the 1989 Annual Report of the Commonwealth Fund.

Families And Aging, A Guide To Legal Concerns, 1988, Extension Circular 1221, Oregon State University Extension Service.

Generations, Spring 1991, Journal Of The American Society On Aging.

Generations, Winter 1992, Journal Of The American Society On Aging.

Growing Old In America, David Hackett Fisher, 1978, Oxford University Press.

How To Live To Be One Hundred Or More, George Burns, 1983, Plume Book.

Incest, A Chilling Report, Lear's, February 1992.

Job Strategies For People With Disabilities, Melanie Astaire Witt, 1992, Peterson's Guides.

Living Arrangements In Later Life, 1989, PNW 318, A Pacific Northwest Extension Publication.

Mirror Mirror, Elissa Malamed, Ph.D., 1983, Linden Press.

New Findings Show Why Employing Workers Over 50 Makes Good Financial Sense For Companies, Released on May 21, 1991, The Commonwealth Fund.

Opportunity 2000, U.S. Department of Labor.

Our Kind, Marvin Harris, 1989, Harper and Row.

Ourselves, Growing Older, Paula Brown Doress and Diana Laskin Siegel and The Midlife And Older Women Book Project, 1987, Touchstone Book.

The New Our Bodies, Ourselves, The Boston Women's Health Book Collective, 1984, Simon and Schuster.

Overcoming Bladder Disorders, Rebecca Chalker and Kristene E. Whitmore, M.D., 1990, Harper and Row.

Perspectives On Aging, Pricilla W. Johnson,
Coordinating Editor, Ballinger Publishing.

Reversing Heart Disease, Dr. Dean Ornish, 1990,
Random House.

Second Careers: New Ways To Work After 50,
Caroline Bird, Little Bown and Company.

The Adult Years, Frederic M. Hudson, 1991,
Jossey-Bass Inc.

The Care And Feeding Of Ideas, James L. Adams,
1986, Addison-Wesley.

*The Human Resource Potential Of American Over
50,* Human Resource Management, Winter 1989.

The Second 50 Years, Walter J. Cheney, William J.
Diehm and Frank E. Seeley, 1992, Paragon House.

The View From 80, Malcolm Cowley, 1980, The
Viking Press.

Truth About Aging, 1986, American Association of
Retired Persons.

Vitality and Aging, James F. Fries and Lawrence M.
Crapo, 1981, W.H. Freeman.

We Live Too Short And Die Too Long, Walter M.
Bortz II, M.D., 1991, Bantam Books.

When Women Retire, Carole Sinclair, 1992, Crown
Publishers.

Why Survive, Robert N. Butler, M.D., 1975, Harper
and Row.

You Can Make A Difference, Marlene Wilson, 1990,
Volunteer Management Associates.

The Third Age
Bookstore
Catalog

A Selected List Of Books
Related To Aging Well

The books briefly reviewed in this section of *Over The Hill At 40 And Other Outrageous Lies* were chosen by the authors for their significance to readers. The object is to bring your attention to nonfiction works of value that can be of direct assistance to you in your planning and pursuit of Third Age activities.

Some of the information you will discover in the books reviewed here has been touched on in the text of *Over The Hill At 40,* but only in a limited way. The books shown here provide a vital resource for the reader who will discover that the Third Age, far from being a period of decline, can be the most exciting era in a mature person's life if he or she takes advantage of the information available to shape and sharpen his or her physical self in a revitalized, energetic frame, leading to increased mental powers and an enhanced zest for living.

The books shown here may be ordered directly from Third Age Press by following the instructions on the book order form located at the back of the book review section.

Over The Hill At 40 And Other Outrageous Lies

Florence and Al Tauber

> HOW TO FEEL 20 TO 30 YEARS
> YOUNGER AT ANY AGE

Over The Hill At 40 And Other Outrageous Lies

Over The Hill At 40 And Other Outrageous Lies, Florence and Al Tauber, Third Age Press, Portland, Oregon 97229— $14.95

In a reportorial style, this collection of facts, predictions, observations, trends and research involving the wave of older people in the United States represents ideas the reader can investigate briefly, then decide to explore more fully in other specialized works related to aging.

In addition to the main text, the book offers a catalog of 14 other works related to aging—a reference library for the mature reader who wants to learn more about the opportunities and the hazards of growing older in the late Twentieth Century.

About the authors: Florence and Al Tauber are a husband and wife team who resent the idea that aging is equated with mental, physical and emotional decline in a youth oriented society that has not come to grips with the fact that older Americans will soon be the dominate age group in the United States.

Age Wave

Age Wave Ken Dychtwald and Joe Flower, Bantam Books, New York, NY, 1990 — $11.95

This book raises questions and suggests consequences about our aging generation that most of us never dreamed of. It points out that the shift to an increasingly larger older population will be unlike any of the experiences faced by prior generations. The 21st Century could be one in which there are Age Wars between the young and old who compete for resources. It asks the question of will we be rich and healthy or poor and sick as a nation? It provokes our imagination and reveals not only concerns about an older populace, but the benefits as well.

The book addresses the enlarging Senior market and the new products and services being developed to satisfy the new demands. In drawing ideas about the future, the book points out that people in their later years become more, not less, diverse and tomorrow's elders will be different, not only from one another, but from today's elders as well. A book that presents the next great social upheaval, *Age Wave* is a glimpse into the future.

About the authors: Ken Dychtwald, Ph.D. is president of Age Wave, Inc. He acts as an advisor to industry and government on the social, lifestyle, and business implications of an aging America.

Joe Flower is an award-winning writer.

Aging On Hold

Aging On Hold, Ronald Kotulak and Peter Gorner, Tribune Publishing, Orlando, Florida, 1992 — $8.95

Aging On Hold is the first book that offers a comprehensive tour of the new frontier of age reversal where researchers boldly endeavor to retard and even reverse human aging, and succeed.

The goal of aging research is to prevent, delay or reverse age-related deficits—to demonstrate methods of avoiding infirmity as long as possible until people expire from truly natural causes after an extended healthy, vigorous life. The discoveries reported in *Aging On Hold* by the authors range from pioneering experiments on the cellular level, to simple techniques that anyone can start using to live longer.

According to the authors, there are three ways of staving off the aging process: lifestyle changes, better diets, exercise and healthier lifestyle and tuneups of bodies and brains by replacing the body's hormones, growth factors, and chemical defense systems. This forseeable development could lead to people routinely living to about 115 years.

The book is a dramatic and intensely interesting read because it confirms the extension of longevity in ways that can be accomplished by science and individuals.

About the authors: Peter Gorner is a Pulitzer Prize winner and is a highly recognized and respected journalist and research writer.

Ronald Kotulak is a science writer for the Chicago Tribune who has been honored by many science organizations.

The Life Plan for
Health and Vitality
in Your Later Years

Aging Well

JAMES F. FRIES, M.D.

Aging Well

Aging Well, James F. Fries, M.D., Addison-Wesley Publishing Company, Inc., New York, NY, 1989 — $14.95

Aging Well which is the title of another book by different authors reviewed here, is a wise and practical guide to successful aging. It offers well tested guidance on every aspect of growing older in good health, and good spirits. As a nationally recognized authority on wellness, Dr. Fries zeros in on attitudes, the value of pride and enthusiasm in preventing disease and maintaining vitality.

He helps the reader learn to cope with everyday problems by encouraging him/her to cast off old stereotypes of helplessness and by maintaining a more positive outlook. As he points out, age may slow us down, but our older years can also be the time of our richest experience, our deepest insights, our most complete individuality.

According to the author, the latest statistics indicate that a 70-year-old woman or man can look forward to another 10 to 15 years of life. That's a long time to waste, or to be uncomfortable because of illness or poor planning. The good news in this book is that you will probably live longer than you think and the best news is that living longer, you can stay vital.

About the author: James F. Fries, M.D., is the author of many books and is an associate professor of Medicine at Stanford University.

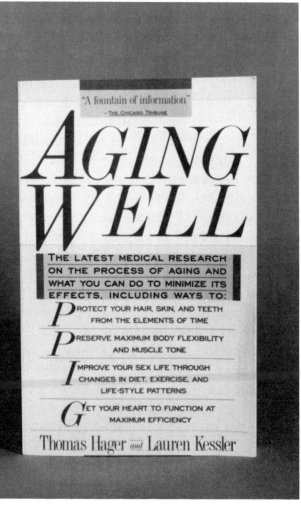

"A fountain of information"
—THE CHICAGO TRIBUNE

AGING WELL

THE LATEST MEDICAL RESEARCH
ON THE PROCESS OF AGING AND
WHAT YOU CAN DO TO MINIMIZE ITS
EFFECTS, INCLUDING WAYS TO:

*P*ROTECT YOUR HAIR, SKIN, AND TEETH
FROM THE ELEMENTS OF TIME

*P*RESERVE MAXIMUM BODY FLEXIBILITY
AND MUSCLE TONE

*I*MPROVE YOUR SEX LIFE THROUGH
CHANGES IN DIET, EXERCISE, AND
LIFE-STYLE PATTERNS

*G*ET YOUR HEART TO FUNCTION AT
MAXIMUM EFFICIENCY

Thomas Hager *and* Lauren Kessler

Aging Well

Aging Well, Thomas Hager and Lauren Kessler, Simon and Shuster, Inc., New York, NY, 1990 — $9.95

A virtual fountain of information, *Aging Well* presents the latest research on the process of aging and what you can do to minimize its effects. It demonstrates ways to protect your hair, skin and teeth, preserve maximum body flexibility and muscle tone, improve your sex life through changes in diet, exercise, and life style patterns and get your heart to function at maximum efficiency.

While we must all face the physical changes that go with aging, there is much we can do to offset the health problems commonly associated with the process. *Aging Well* offers practical, informative ways to wear your years gracefully and it provides answers to how aging causes changes in our hair, our eyes, our bodies. These events are explained in instructive detail and what happens to us physically and mentally is explored and information on how to retard deterioration is outlined.

About the authors: Thomas Hager holds degrees in medical microbiology and journalism and is a correspondent for *American Health.*

Lauren Kessler writes on health issues for *US, Self, Spring* and *Northwest Magazine.*

BIOMARKERS
THE
10
DETERMINANTS OF AGING
YOU CAN CONTROL
A medically proven
program that can slow down
the aging process and add
renewed strength and vitality
to your life—
no matter what your age!
WILLIAM EVANS, PH.D., AND IRWIN H. ROSENBERG, M.D.
PROFESSORS OF NUTRITION AND MEDICINE, TUFTS UNIVERSITY
WITH JACQUELINE THOMPSON

Biomarkers

Biomarkers, William Evans and Irwin H. Rosenberg, M.D., Simon and Shuster, New York, NY, 1991 — $21.95

This book presents a medically proven program that shows the reader how to control the aging process. Based on research that proves aging is not an irreversible process but one that responds dynamically to exercise and diet, *Biomarkers,* will help you double your energy and feel terrific, not for a day, or a week, but for a lifetime. The most exciting news of all is that the 10 key physiological factors associated with aging, called Biomarkers, are controllable regardless of your age or present physical condition.

The authors demonstrate how the reader can measure his own Bio-Status and assess his aerobic capacity. Encouraging is the information that "Aging Schedules" are as individual as people are. Aging is not something that happens suddenly. The pace of aging varies enormously from one person to the next and to a great extent it can be controlled by the individual.

The paramount message in the book is that readers who complete the programs described will reach new peaks in fitness levels.

About the authors: William J. Evans, Ph. D. is chief of the Human Physiology Laboratory at the HNRCA and is exercise advisor of the Boston Bruins and the New England Patriots.

Irwin H. Rosenberg, M.D., is a director of the USDA Human Nutrition Center on Aging at Tufts University.

How to take full advantage of the AMERICANS WITH DISABILITIES ACT

Job Strategies for People with Disabilities

- *Uncovering marketable skills, step-by-step*
- *Standout resumes and successful interviews*
- *How to make the job you want fit you*

"The single best career guide ever written for people with disabilities."
—Joyce Lain Kennedy
Nationally Syndicated Careers Columnist

Melanie Astaire Witt

Job Strategies For People With Disabilities

Job Strategies For People With Disabilities, Melanie Astaire Witt, Peterson's Guides, Princeton, NJ, 1992 — $14.95

The new Americans with Disabilities Act (ADA) opens doors of opportunity never before available to the disabled, as this definitive career book points out. It is full of sensitive and practical advice for getting the first job, being promoted, and making career changes. It answers the questions about the law, career decision-making and job finding. The book tells stories of real people with real jobs and they share their secrets of success.

If you are disabled and aspire to be a member of the world of work this book offers ways to explore your good worker skills, redesign your resume, take stock of your skills and recognize your potential for success. It points out that limitations are not stop signs, they are yellow yield signals. It encourages you to enable yourself for today's job market.

About the author: Melanie Astaire Witt is a career journalist who has family members who have experienced several disabilities. She is a regular contributor to *Career World.*

OURSELVES, GROWING OLDER

By Paula Brown Doress and
Diana Laskin Siegal and
The Midlife and
Older Women Book Project

In cooperation with
The Boston Women's Health
Book Collective, authors of
The New Our Bodies, Ourselves

WOMEN AGING WITH
KNOWLEDGE AND POWER

Ourselves, Growing Older

Ourselves, Growing Older, Paula Brown Doress, Diana Laskin Siegal and The Midlife and Older Women Book Project, Simon and Shuster, New York, NY, 1987 — $18.00

A health and living handbook for older women, this comprehensive work presents a positive approach to physical and emotional health. It probably contains the most frank and complete information available on older woman's health care issues. As such, it is an invitation to women to assume responsibility for their own bodies.

The focus is on a wide variety of topics that include aging and well being, body image assessment, childbearing at midlife, sexuality in middle and later years, menopause, entering the Third Age, coping with the medical care system, living and housing alternatives, as well as work, retirement and money matters.

Ourselves Growing Up is an authoritative guide that deals with habits that need changing, offers methods, help and support groups and offers solid information about foiling the beauty business myths.

Many women participated in the research and writing of this book and as a result it offers the reader a strong female viewpoint and the company of many like herself who are learning to celebrate their Third Age femaleness.

About the authors: Paula Brown Doress and Diana Laskin Siegal and the Middle and Older Women Book Project in cooperation with the Boston Women's Health Book Collective are also authors of *The New Our Bodies, Ourselves.*

THE NEW
OUR BODIES, OURSELVES

*A Book By and
For Women*

*By The Boston
Women's Health
Book Collective*

WOMEN
UNITE

The New Our Bodies, Ourselves

The New Our Bodies, Ourselves, Boston Women's Health Book Collective, Simon and Shuster, New York, NY 1984 — $17.95

This book, called "The most important work to come out of the woman's movement" is a completely new version of the original that influenced the thinking of a generation of women and men. Written by the Boston Women's Health Book Collective, it breaks ground courageously by discussing difficult problems and providing the most complete source book available on women's health care issues.

There is new information and the most current thinking on every topic covered in the original book. New chapters have been included on body image, alcohol, mood altering drugs, and smoking. Alternatives to medical care, health and healing, psychotherapy, environmental and occupational health, violence against women, new reproductive technologies, women growing older, developing an international awareness, and other topics make the book an outstanding resource.

It is a topical reference to guide the reader to the appropriate resource on any subject about women's health care she may wish to enquire into.

About the authors: The Boston Women's Health Book Collective is a group of women dedicated to the dissemination of information to women on all matters relating to a woman's well being.

OVERCOMING BLADDER DISORDERS

Compassionate, Authoritative Medical
and Self-help Solutions for

Incontinence
Cystitis
Interstitial Cystitis
Prostate Problems
Bladder Cancer

REBECCA CHALKER &
KRISTENE E. WHITMORE, M.D.

"This book is the best resource any patient with a bladder problem could ever hope to find....I highly recommend it as a resource for both patients and health professionals." —Suzanne Frye, M.D., Division of Urology, The New York Hospital, Cornell Medical Center

Overcoming Bladder Disorders

Overcoming Bladder Disorders by Rebecca Chalker and Kristene E. Whitmore, M.D., Harper and Row Publishers, New York, NY, 1990 — $9.95

An informative and positive book directed at a problem that is seldom openly discussed. The book offers practical self help solutions for bladder and incontinence problems. This is a must book, particularly for women who suffer bladder weakness and the embarrassment that goes with it. Causes of incontinence are explained, cures are explored and strategies for coping are reviewed.

The book explains how to understand the relevant physiology of the incontinence, how to evaluate diagnostic procedures, find a sympathetic, informed source of treatment. It shows how to locate support groups and overcome the emotional and sexual impact.

All areas of bladder disorders of men and women are described in detail, with information on treatment, cures, and coping. Bladder disorders present enormous challenges to both patient and health care professionals who treat them, but the good news is the majority of the problems are manageable.

About the authors: Kristene E. Whitmore, M.D., is clinical associate professor of Urology at the University of Pennsylvania and director of Urology of the Incontinence Center at Graduate Hospital in Philadelphia.

Rebecca Chalker is author and editor of *A New View Of A Woman's Body* and *How To Stay Out Of The Gynecologist's Office.*

Dr. DEAN ORNISH'S
PROGRAM FOR
REVERSING
HEART DISEASE

The Only
System
Scientifically
Proven to
Reverse
Heart Disease
Without
Drugs or
Surgery

Dr. Dean Ornish's Program
For Reversing Heart Disease

Dr. Dean Ornish's Program For Reversing Heart Disease, Random House, New York, NY, 1990 — $24.95

This is a ground breaking book that demonstrates that even severe coronary heart disease can be reversed. It illustrates that when we begin healing our lives, our hearts heal as well. Dr. Ornish's program can lead to a better life as well as a longer one. It is the only program scientifically validated to begin reversing even severe heart disease. More than a book on reversing heart disease, it is a powerful and wise prescription for opening the heart in the deepest sense. It is an affirmation of the best of what medicine has to offer. You don't have to have heart disease to be healed through this program.

This book is about how to enjoy living, not how to avoid dying; how to relax, how to manage stress, not how to avoid it; how to live in the world more fully, not how to withdraw from it; and how to take care of yourself so that you can give more fully to others.

Dr. Ornish's book presents the first scientific proof that it is possible to actually reverse heart disease without drugs or surgery. Based on 13 years of research, the book presents astonishing conclusions about reversing or preventing heart disease by simply changing your lifestyle.

About the author: Dean Ornish, M.D., is assistant clinical professor of Medicine and Attending Physician at the School of Medicine, University of California, San Francisco.

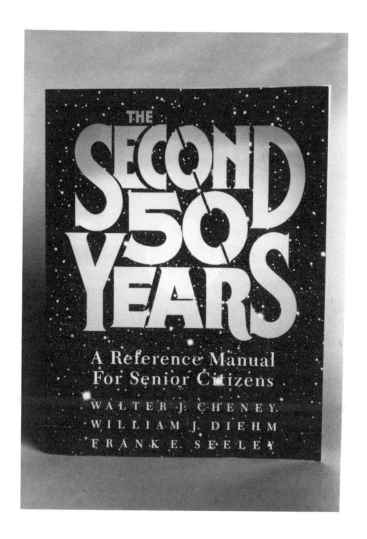

The Second 50 Years

The Second 50 Years, Walter J. Cheney, William J. Diehm, and Frank E. Seeley, Paragon House, New York, NY, 1992 — $21.95

This book is a reference manual for Senior Citizens, a one-stop, total-life resource packed with solid advice, ideas, suggestions and warnings. It contains practical information on how you can live a happy, healthy, productive life in spite of the changes that come with growing older.

If you are a Senior, family member, friend or professional who deals with Seniors, this book will provide you with a detailed look at hundred of critical issues including, Senior rights, insurance, creative retirement, health and diet, housing, finance, medical issues, grandparenting, safety and security, medications, living alone, driving, consumer rights, travel, and addresses and phone numbers for Senior organizations, mutual help groups, agencies and more. This book is for you if you are one of the 66 million Americans 50 and over. In the more than 425 oversize, easy-to-read pages, you'll find the tools to make a wonderful life for yourself and those you love.

The authors wrote this manual in the hope that it will help you face retirement with the greatest strength and that you will find happiness and fulfillment in spite of the adversities of life.

About the authors: Walter Cheney, William Diehm and Frank Seeley, as Seniors themselves, realized that problems become less formidable if we educate ourselves on conditions we face as we grow older.

Vitality and Aging

Vitality and Aging, James Fries and Lawrence Crapo, W. H. Freeman and Company, San Francisco, California, 1981 — $14.95

All of us can be healthier and more vital in later age, say the authors of this book, which presents optimistic and realistic predictions based on a new synthesis of information on human aging. The book shows how an increase in the vitality of the elderly can be predicted from current health trends. As a result, it offers the hope to older readers for a meaningful kind of rejuvenation where the maximum life span is not prolonged but the period of vitality is.

About the authors: Dr. James F. Fries is associate professor at Stanford University School of Medicine where he is active in the field of medical self care.

Dr. Lawrence M. Crapo is clinical director of the Geriatric Research Center at the Veterans Medical Center in Palo Alto, California and is an assistant professor at Stanford University School of Medicine. He is the recipient of a Geriatric Medicine Academic Award from the National Institute of Aging.

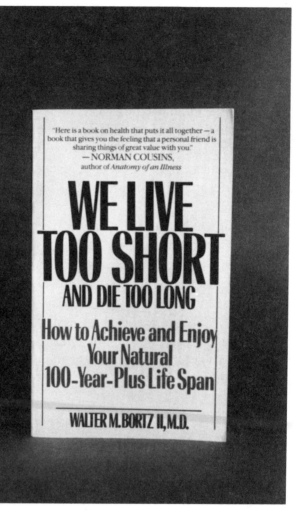

"Here is a book on health that puts it all together — a book that gives you the feeling that a personal friend is sharing things of great value with you."
— NORMAN COUSINS,
author of *Anatomy of an Illness*

WE LIVE TOO SHORT
AND DIE TOO LONG

How to Achieve and Enjoy Your Natural 100-Year-Plus Life Span

WALTER M. BORTZ II, M.D.

We Live Too Short And Die Too Long

We Live Too Short And Die Too Long, Walter M. Bortz II, M.D., Bantam Books, New York, NY, 1991 — $12.00

In his book, Dr. Bortz sets out the elements for longevity with effective dynamic strategies to help you prevent premature death. You can start today to gain decades of active, satisfying living if you follow the basic practices he outlines, no matter what your age. His program of eight simple directives includes physiological goals that provide the reader with the ability to live more years, more fully that it was thought possible. He points out lucidly that we now know there is nothing magical or mysterious about life and youth extension. .

He points out that the aging person must evaluate the prospects and determine the price he is willing to pay for a more vital and joyous Third Age. It is not a price that is beyond the ability of the average person who wants enriched years of later life.

New frontiers in the science of aging studies are opening every day and life extension becomes more real, Dr. Bortz says, making the future an exciting one for Third Age members.

About the author: Walter M. Bortz II, M.D., is one of America's most acclaimed authorities on aging. He is former president of the American Geriatrics Society and has over 35 years of clinical experience. He is presently clinical associate professor at Stanford University Medical School.

WHEN WOMEN RETIRE

CAROLE SINCLAIR

THE PROBLEMS THEY FACE & HOW TO SOLVE THEM

When Women Retire

When Women Retire, Carole Sinclair, Crown Publishers, New York, NY, 1992 — $20.00

Retirement of women presents new challenges, says the author. It is not an idyllic time of leisure and relaxation. New issues of reduced health care, lack of benefits, dependent spouses, children and grand children and sometimes parents, occupy the woman who has reached an older age.

One of the pertinent questions asked and addressed in the book is how does a woman who never worked outside the home support herself?

The book is a personal reference that will enable the reader to take charge of her life and lifestyle and help keep her stable during times of trying economic adjustment. But the author points out that retirement is not the end of the road. It can be a time for exploration of paths not travelled before, of opportunities not noticed or taken advantage of. The retirement years can be a time for self fulfillment and happiness.

The insistent theme of the book is that the Third Age can be a new chapter in a woman's life, a clean slate, with her being the author of what is written on it from now on. She must develop an open mind with a new attitude of retiring to a new future rather than retiring from an old one.

This is a helping book that shows the reader how to help herself to know the problems she faces and how to solve them.

About the author: Carole Sinclair is a lecturer on all aspects of women in business.

The Authors

Florence and Al Tauber are a husband and wife team who has worked together closely during a 40-year marriage to make successful several entrepreneurial ventures which led them into startup companies for computer retrieval systems, airline reservations, and automatic imaging systems. A mechanical and industrial engineer, Al Tauber, strongly supported by Florence, became an internationally recognized expert in systems analysis and design, product development and strategic planning.

While *Over The Hill At 40 And Other Outrageous Lies* is the first publicly offered book jointly authored by Florence and Al, the couple has collaborated in public speaking and in marketing design studies. Al is a fellow of the Association of Information and Image Management and has taught document storage and retrieval at UCLA and the AIIM Institute.

Inspiration for their book came from the couple's own experiences as mature individuals who realized that Third Age Americans have not been educated about the immense changes that are challenging the United States as millions of citizens reach senior status with little social planning to welcome their entry into the older years.

Special Sales

Over The Hill At 40 And Other Outrageous Lies is available at special quantity discounts for bulk purchases for sales promotions, premiums or fund raising. Special books or book excerpts can also be created to fit specific needs. Write:

Special Sales Department
THIRD AGE PRESS
1075 N.W. Murray Road, Suite 277
Portland, Oregon 97229
Phone: 503-690-3251

ORDER FORM RECOMMENDED BOOKS

Qty	Title	Price	Total
[ ]	Over The Hill At 40 And Other Outrageous Lies,	$14.95	_____
[ ]	Age Wave	$11.95	_____
[ ]	Aging On Hold	$8.95	_____
[ ]	Aging Well, Fries	$14.95	_____
[ ]	Aging Well, Hager	$9.95	_____
[ ]	Biomarkers	$21.95	_____
[ ]	Job Strategies For People With Disabilities	$14.95	_____
[ ]	Ourselves, Growing Older,	$18.00	_____
[ ]	Our Bodies, Ourselves, The New	$17.95	_____
[ ]	Overcoming Bladder Disorders	$9.95	_____
[ ]	Reversing Heart Disease	$24.95	_____
[ ]	Second 50 Years, The	$21.95	_____
[ ]	Vitality and Aging	$14.95	_____
[ ]	We Live Too Short And Die Too Long	$12.00	_____
[ ]	When Women Retire	$20.00	_____

THIRD AGE PRESS
1075 N.W. Murray Rd, Ste. 277
Portland, Oregon 97229
Fax 503-645-5040
Phone 503-690-3251 or 800-VITAL AGE

Total For Books: _____
Shipping & Handling: _____
Order Total: _____

Shipping and handling $3.00 for the first book, $1.00 for each additional book processed with the same order.

I understand that I may return any book for a full refund, for any reason, no questions asked.

[ ] Please place my name on your mailing list.

[ ] I would be interested in subscribing to a newsletter that keeps me informed on Third Age developments.

Name _____

Address _____

City/State/Zip _____

Phone _____ MC VISA

Credit Card No _____ Exp. Date _____

Signature _____